CHRISTIAN BEGINNINGS

IS VOLUME

74

OF THE

Twentieth Century Encyclopedia of Catholicism

UNDER SECTION

VII

THE HISTORY OF THE CHURCH

IT IS ALSO THE

54TH

VOLUME IN ORDER OF PUBLICATION

Edited by HENRI DANIEL-ROPS of the Académie Française

CHRISTIAN BEGINNINGS

By JACQUES ZEILLER

Translated by P. J. HEPBURNE-SCOTT

HAWTHORN BOOKS · PUBLISHERS · *New York*

67246

First Edition, November, 1960

NIHIL OBSTAT

Rt. Rev. Msgr. Joseph H. Brady, S.T.D.

 Censor Librorum

IMPRIMATUR

Most Reverend Thomas A. Boland, S.T.D.

 Archbishop of Newark

Newark, November 28, 1960

BR
165
Z413
c1

CONTENTS

THE PREACHING OF THE CROSS FROM PENTECOST TO THE COMPLETION OF THE APOSTOLIC WRITINGS

Christ has sometimes been called a revolutionary. The term, with all its implications of violence and rupture with the past, is hardly appropriate. Yet it is true that his message was bound to bring about a revolution, for it called men to a completely new kind of life, in which each was to live for all, not for himself. With him, charity, in the fullest meaning of the word, entered a world which had never known it. So unheard-of an appeal was bound to provoke surprise, mistrust, resistance and even formidable hostility, but in spite of everything it was victorious, and the first striking thing about it is the speed of its propagation.

Jesus said that he himself was sent only to the lost sheep of the house of Israel. But immediately after his resurrection he charged his apostles with the spiritual conquest of the world, and they lost no time in embarking on it.

They had to begin, however, with those nearest at hand. No sooner were the apostles filled with the Holy Ghost on the day of Pentecost than they addressed the Jews of Jerusalem, and the first sermon of Peter, their head, produced more than three thousand converts, to be followed almost at once by others.

Almost at once, too, began the conflict with the religious authorities of Judaism, the men who could not tolerate the preaching of Christ. The apostles were flogged and imprisoned. When released, they began again at once. Nothing could stop them.

But not only was the faith of Christ being spread: charity too was being practised. From the beginning the faithful held everything in common; those who had property sold it and shared the price among all, so that none were in need (Acts 4. 34), the apostles distributing the proceeds of the sales according to every man's need. But as the numbers of the converts continued to grow, especially with the arrival of Jews from outside Palestine, complaints began to be made, the newcomers considering themselves worse treated than the others. So for this daily distribution the apostles appointed seven men who could spend most of their time on it, while they themselves could be occupied entirely with prayer and the ministry of the word (Acts 6. 4). These ministers of charity were the deacons. But they did not give up proclaiming the Good News, the "Gospel," and Stephen, their leader, did so with such success that the enemies of Christ's teaching stoned him to death.

This was the signal for an outburst of hostility against the infant Church of Jerusalem, only the apostles daring to stay in the city. This dispersal was of great benefit, as it contributed powerfully to the spread of the gospel.

Philip the Deacon evangelized Samaria and then the whole region of Caesarea, after converting, near Gaza, a proselyte Jew of Ethiopia, an official of the queen of that country. Soon there were followers of Christ in Damascus, in Syria, possibly converted from among the Essenes, Israelites professing a purer faith than the Sadducees and with a less legalistic ideal of justice than the Pharisees. The discovery of the Dead Sea scrolls in our day has made them the object of earnest if not always revealing study.

This name of Damascus sprang suddenly into prominence in the history of the infant Church. Hearing that the new faith had reached this city, Saul of Tarsus, one of its bitterest opponents, who had been a willing witness of Stephen's murder, obtained authority for a mission of inquiry and punishment. But on his journey the grace of Christ struck him down, and when he had heard him whom henceforth, like the apostles, he owned as Lord, he became in a moment his most ardent disciple.

Hardly had this unique recruit been received from the Jews when Peter introduced to the Church the first pagan, the Roman centurion Cornelius, whom he baptized without obliging him first to become a Jew.

But already the faithful had carried the word to Phoenicia, Cyprus and the great city of Antioch, where for the first time the disciples of Christ were called Christians. Saul, henceforth known as Paul (his name as a Roman citizen), and Barnabas, the companion he took with him, soon came there and conversions multiplied. The movement never looked back again.

There was, however, a question of some gravity which had to be faced if progress was not to be compromised. Christians of Jewish origin who came to Antioch maintained that converts from paganism ought to conform to Jewish laws, such as circumcision and abstention from certain foods. The matter seemed important enough to justify a meeting of the apostles at Jerusalem, later known as the Council of Jerusalem. The obligation of circumcision was rejected. So as not to offend the others, converts from paganism were only required to refrain from eating the flesh of animals slaughtered in ways that shocked them. Inevitably a prohibition of this nature soon disappeared. Only one command remained, and that permanently, for it was of a quite different order; that forbidding sexual impurity.

The fusion of the two heterogeneous elements was thus made easy. The Gentiles could now enter the Church without first becoming Jews.

Above all others it was Paul who was called by his vocation to win the "nations" to the faith on an equality with the children of Israel. In the course of three missions, —from A.D. 44 to 49, from 53 to 55 and then, apparently, from 55 to 58—he was led to Cyprus and into several regions of Asia Minor; Pamphylia, Pisidia and Lycaonia; then crossing to Europe he went to Macedonia, where he evangelized Philippi, Thessalonica, Athens (where the sceptics mocked him when he spoke of the resurrection), Corinth, then back into Asia Minor, where he reached Galatia and Phrygia; once again to Greece and Macedonia and at least the frontiers of Illyricum. Everywhere his preaching was successful, since even in Athens, where rationalism prevailed, he made conversions among the élite, such as Dionysius the Areopagite.

But also, as was inevitable, he provoked contradiction and reaction. Judaism was as hostile as ever. In Jerusalem the apostle James, brother of John, was put to death by Herod, "to please the Jews," and for a second time Peter was put in prison and miraculously set free.

But even within the bounds of the young Church there were frictions, to say the least, between Jewish Christians and those from the Gentiles, who were becoming more numerous. It was at Antioch that a famous incident occurred, related by St Paul. The Judaizers, holding to their old customs, abstained from certain foods. Not so the others. Paul, who had realized at once that the external links between Christianity and Judaism had to disappear, boldly sat down at their table. Peter, arriving in due course at Antioch, at first copied him but, in face of criticism from the opposite party, soon ceased to do so, for which Paul, to win him back, did not hesitate to "rebuke" him firmly.

But in the end he himself was arrested in his triumphant career. Scarcely had he returned to Jerusalem from his apostolic journeys, during which he had not only preached the gospel but confirmed the faith of the believers by numerous letters, to the Romans, the Corinthians, the Galatians and others, when he was cast into prison. So furious were the Jews against the "apostate" that his life was threatened. To avoid an act of violence Lysias, the representative of the Roman authority, secured his person and sent him to Felix, the procurator at Caesarea. But Paul, invoking his rights as a Roman citizen, appealed to the emperor and eventually arrived under guard at Rome. There he found some Christians, with whom he had already been in touch through his letters. As a prisoner, not closely confined but accessible, he was able to continue his teaching. This arrival at Rome really crowned his apostolic career, though it certainly did not end it.

He was probably set at liberty and then achieved his desire to reach the bounds of the west, that is, Spain, with perhaps a visit (though this is pure conjecture) to the Mediterranean coast of Gaul. He could then say—though obviously this must not be taken literally—that the word of God had "gone forth to the whole world."

There were other messengers too. Peter and Paul's activities were mutually complementary. For Peter, Antioch was only a temporary stage. He in turn toured some of the provinces of Asia Minor, as seems to be indicated in the Epistles which bears his name, and stayed at Corinth. He too arrived in Rome, at a date which cannot be determined. The fourfold testimony of second-century writers (St Ignatius of Antioch, St Clement of Alexandria, St Dionysius of Corinth and St Irenaeus of Lyons) and, earlier, of St Clement of Rome, an allusion in I Peter, the tradition recorded in the second century that Rome preserved the "trophies," that is, the relics of Peter and Paul, and finally the decisive excavations carried out in our days under St Peter's Basilica, all these leave no reasonable doubt as to the final presence of St Peter in Rome. The concordant testimonies of St Clement of Rome and Tertullian are definite as to the martyrdom which ended his apostolic labours in the City which this presence made for ever the centre of the Church.

Thus, a quarter of a century after the death of Christ, his word, through his apostles, had reached the centre of the Roman world. If some "traditions," too late to be accepted, attribute spheres of activity, sometimes very distant, to various apostles (though such statements require considerable reserve), it is certain that one or more Christian communities were founded in Persia in the apostolic age, and though it is impossible to assign even an approximate date to the first Christian preaching in India or at least its immediate approaches, it must be granted that the evangelization of this part of the world dates from very early antiquity. In another direction, we find the memory of the evangelist St Mark, St Peter's disciple, in the origins of the Church of Egypt.

Thus, by the end of the first century the greater part of the Mediterranean world had heard of Christ, and his message had been proclaimed in the interior of Asia.

By the design of Providence the Roman empire became the chief theatre of the early evangelization of the world, but in its turn the former empire of Alexander, stretching farther to the east, began to be opened to the Gospel.

This message of Christ was a message proclaimed by men in public places, like St Paul at Athens or in the Jewish synagogues, and probably also in more private gatherings. But several added to this their written teaching.

In the course of his ceaseless journeys, St Paul found time to address letters to the Churches he had founded and sometimes to others which he approached spontaneously, like that of Rome, in order to renew his preaching, to clarify a point of doctrine or morals, to call the erring to order or to settle quarrels, for quarrels there were from the outset, as inevitably there always would be. His famous Epistles to the Romans, the Corinthians, the Galatians and others are the oldest written documents of Christian tradition. St Peter too wrote, though less copiously, and others, like James, the first head of the Jerusalem community, and Jude, of whom nothing else is known.

Thus, little by little, was formed what was to become the New Testament, the sequel to the Old, which was made up of the sacred books of the Hebrews. But the actual records of the life and sayings of Christ, which eventually became the first books of these new Scriptures, were not the first to see the light. The memoirs of the life and deeds of Jesus, the *Logia* of Christ, were at first transmitted orally. But the time soon came when it was felt necessary to have them written down: the task was undertaken by eyewitnesses, either actual apostles or disciples, and thus were born the four Gospels, which were given the names of the apostle Matthew, of Peter's disciple Mark, of Luke, Paul's physician and faithful companion, and finally of John, who in his last years completed their important work by writing or prompting the composition of the Fourth Gospel, the "spiritual" Gospel. This recorded not so much the actions as the words of our Lord, and perhaps even more than his words (especially those whose deeper meaning had at first escaped most of his hearers and had not been written down), the ineffable truths which they signified.

The Acts of the Apostles, the natural complement of the Gospels, earlier than the Fourth Gospel but later than that of Luke, whose purpose was to give it a sequel in these Acts, are *par excellence* the history of the early days of the Church, and are full of priceless information. We could wish that this were even fuller and more circumstantial than it is, but more than once it is opportunely supplemented by the Epistles. The significant but happily resolved dispute, for example, which momentarily divided St Peter and St Paul at Antioch, is related much more explicitly in one of St Paul's Epistles than in the Acts.

The series of canonical books, those, that is, which the Church receives as faithful interpreters of her thought, without necessarily guaranteeing the historical accuracy of the traditional names of their authors, is completed by the mysterious Apocalypse of St. John. It is, so to speak, the vision and prophecy of the future destiny, the trials and triumphs, of the Christian faith. In this book it is quite useless to try to find, after the event, a prophecy of future events, with naïve precision of detail, based on our knowledge of them as past events, perhaps through an unconscious desire to discover the outlines of future history under the mystery of these prophecies.

However comforting these prophecies may prove to Christians today, it is not they which make the New Testament so precious to its readers, but the direct contact it gives with Jesus himself, whom Christians have always longed to know ever more fully. This was early proved by a crop of apocryphal books, in which legendary tales, miracles more startling than edifying, and even bad taste, contrast so startlingly with the sober discretion of the Gospels. But we also find in the reading of the canonical texts the main features of the life of the infant Church, concerning which practically everything we can now know is preserved in the Acts and the apostolic Epistles.

CONTEMPORARY DOCUMENTS

THE LIFE OF THE PRIMITIVE COMMUNITY

These documents continually discussed with the apostles' teaching, their fellowship in the breaking of bread, and the fixed times of prayer, and every soul was struck with awe, so many were the wonders and signs performed by the apostles in Jerusalem. All the faithful held together, and shared all they had, selling their possessions and their means of livelihood, so as to distribute to all, as each had need. They persevered with one accord, day by day, in the temple worship, and, as they broke bread in this house or that, took their share of food with gladness and simplicity of heart, praising God, and winning favour with all the people. And each day the Lord added to their fellowship others that were to be saved. (Acts 2. 42-7.)

There was one heart and soul in all the company of believers; none of them called any of his possessions his own, everything was shared in common. Great was the power with which the apostles testified to the resurrection of our Lord Jesus Christ, and great was the grace that rested on them all. None of them was destitute; all those who owned farms or houses used to sell them, and bring the price of what they had sold to lay it at the apostles' feet, so that each could have what share of it he needed. There was a Levite called Joseph, a Cypriot by birth, to whom the apostles gave the fresh name of Barnabas, which means the man of encouragement; he had an estate, which he sold, and brought the purchase-money to lay it at the apostles' feet. (Acts 4. 32-7.)

THE QUESTION OF THE JUDAIZERS:
THE COUNCIL OF JERUSALEM

The issue

Some visitors came down from Judæa, who began to tell the brethren, You cannot be saved without being circumcised according to the tradition of Moses. Paul and Barnabas were drawn into a great controversy with them; and it was decided that Paul and Barnabas and certain of the rest should go up to see the apostles and presbyters in Jerusalem about this question. So the church saw them on their way, and they passed through Phoenice and Samaria, relating how the Gentiles were turning to God, and so brought great rejoicing to all the brethren. When they reached Jerusalem, they were welcomed by the church, and by the apostles and presbyters; and they told them of all that God had done to aid them. But some believers who belonged to the party of the Pharisees came forward and declared, They must be circumcised; we must call upon them to keep the law of Moses.

The apostles and presbyters deliberate

When the apostles and presbyters assembled to decide about this matter there was much disputing over it, until Peter rose and said to them, Brethren, you know well enough how from early days it has been God's choice that the Gentiles should hear the message of the gospel from my lips, and so learn to believe. God, who can read men's hearts, has assured them of his favour by giving the Holy Spirit to them as to us. He would not make any difference between us and them; he had removed all the uncleanness from their hearts when he gave them faith. How is it, then, that you would now call God in question, by putting a yoke on the necks of the disciples, such

as we and our fathers have been too weak to bear?
It is by the grace of our Lord Jesus Christ that we hope
to be saved, and they no less. Then the whole company
kept silence, and listened to Barnabas and Paul describing
all the signs and wonders God had performed among the
Gentiles by their means.

And when they had finished speaking, James answered
thus, Listen, brethren, to what I have to say. Simon has
told us, how for the first time God has looked with favour
on the Gentiles, and chosen from among them a people
dedicated to his name. This is in agreement with the words
of the prophets, where it is written: Afterwards, I will
come back, and build up again David's tabernacle that
has fallen; I will build up its ruins, and raise it afresh;
so that all the rest of mankind may find the Lord, all
those Gentiles among whom my name is named, says the
Lord, who is the doer of all this. God has known from all
eternity what he does today. And so I give my voice for
sparing the consciences of those Gentiles who have found
their way to God; only writing to bid them abstain from
what is contaminated by idolatry, from fornication, and
from meat which has been strangled or has the blood in it.
As for Moses, ever since the earliest times he has been
read, sabbath after sabbath, in the synagogues, and has
preachers in every city to expound him.

The decision and decree

Thereupon it was resolved by the apostles and presbyters, with the agreement of the whole church, to chose
out some of their own number and despatch them to
Antioch with Paul and Barnabas; namely, Judas who was
called Barsabas, and Silas, who were leading men among
the brethren. And they sent, by their hands, this message
in writing:

To the Gentile brethren in Antioch, Syria and Cilicia,

their brethren the apostles and presbyters send greeting. We hear that some of our number who visited you have disquieted you by what they said, unsettling your consciences, although we had given them no such commission; and therefore, meeting together with common purpose of heart, we have resolved to send you chosen messengers, in company with our well-beloved Barnabas and Paul, men who have staked their lives for the name of our Lord Jesus Christ. We have given this commission to Judas and Silas, who will confirm the message by word of mouth. It is the Holy Spirit's pleasure and ours that no burden should be laid upon you beyond these, which cannot be avoided; you are to abstain from what is sacrificed to idols, from blood-meat and meat which has been strangled, and from fornication. If you keep away from such things, you will have done your part. Farewell.

So they took their leave and went down to Antioch, where they called the multitude together and delivered the letter to them; and they, upon reading it, were rejoiced at this encouragement. Judas and Silas, for they were prophets too, said much to encourage the brethren and establish their faith; they stayed there for some time before the brethren let them go home, in peace, to those who had sent them. (But Silas had a mind to remain there; so Judas went back alone to Jerusalem.) Paul and Barnabas waited at Antioch, teaching and preaching God's word with many others to help them. (Acts 15. 1-36.)

ST PAUL'S ACCOUNT

Paul did not receive his Gospel
from men, but from God

Let me tell you this, brethren; the gospel I preached to you is not a thing of man's dictation; it was not from man that I inherited or learned it, it came to me by a revelation from Jesus Christ. You have been told how I bore myself in my Jewish days, how I persecuted God's Church beyond measure and tried to destroy it, going further in my zeal as a Jew than many of my own age and race, so fierce a champion was I of the traditions handed down from my forefathers. And then, he who had set me apart from the day of my birth, and called me by his grace, saw fit to make his Son known in me, so that I could preach his gospel among the Gentiles. My first thought was not to hold any consultations with any human creature; I did not go up to Jerusalem to see those who had been apostles longer than myself; no, I went off into Arabia, and when I came back, it was to Damascus. Then, when three years had passed, I did go up to Jerusalem, to visit Peter, and I stayed a fortnight there in his company; but I did not see any other of the apostles, except James, the Lord's brother. Such is my history; as God sees me, I am telling you the plain truth. Afterwards, I travelled into other parts of the world, Syria and Cilicia; and all the time I was not even known by sight to the Christian churches of Judaea; they only knew by hearsay, "the man who used to persecute us is now preaching the faith he once tried to destroy," and they praised God for what he had done in me.

Paul's gospel received the approval
of the other apostles

Then, after an interval of fourteen years, once again I went up to Jerusalem with Barnabas; and Titus also accompanied me. I went up in obedience to a revelation, and there I communicated to them (only in private, to men of repute) the gospel I always preach among the Gentiles; was it possible that the course I had taken and was taking was useless? And it is not even true to say that they insisted on my companion Titus, who was a Greek, being circumcised; we were only thinking of those false brethren who had insinuated themselves into our company so as to spy on the liberty which we enjoy in Christ Jesus, meaning to make slaves of us. To these we did not give ground for a moment by way of obedience; we were resolved that the true principles of the gospel should remain undisturbed in your possession. But as for what I owe to those who were of some repute—it matters little to me who or what they were, God makes no distinction between man and man—these men of repute, I say, had nothing to communicate to me. On the contrary, those who were reputed to be the main support of the Church, James and Cephas and John, saw plainly that I was commissioned to preach to the uncircumcised, as Peter was to the circumcised; he whose power had enabled Peter to become the apostle of the circumcised, had enabled me to become the apostle of the Gentiles. And so, recognising the grace God had given me, they joined their right hands in fellowship with Barnabas and myself; the Gentiles were to be our province, the circumcised theirs. Only we were to remember the poor; which was the very thing I had set myself to do.

The incident at Antioch

Afterwards, when Cephas came to Antioch, I opposed him openly; he stood self-condemned. He had been eating with the Gentiles, until we were visited by certain delegates from James; but when these came, he began to draw back and hold himself aloof, overawed by the supporters of circumcision. The rest of the Jews were no less false to their principles; Barnabas himself was carried away by their insincerity. So, when I found that they were not following the true path of the gospel, I said to Cephas in front of them all, Since thou, who art a born Jew, dost follow the Gentile, not the Jewish way of life, by what right dost thou bind the Gentiles to live like Jews? We are Jews by right of nature, we do not come from the guilty stock of the Gentiles; yet we found out that it is through faith in Jesus Christ, not by obeying the law, that a man is justified. We, like anyone else, had to learn to believe in Jesus Christ, so that we might be justified by faith in Christ, not by observance of the law. Observance of the law cannot win acceptance for a single human creature.

By putting our hopes of justification in Christ, we took our rank as guilty creatures like the rest. Does that mean that Christ brings us guilt? That is not to be thought of: do I put myself in the wrong, when I destroy and then rebuild? Through the law, my old self has become dead to the law, so that I may live to God; with Christ I hang upon the cross, and yet I am alive; or rather, not I; it is Christ that lives in me. True, I am living, here and now, this mortal life; but my real life is the faith I have in the Son of God, who loved me, and gave himself for me. I do not spurn the grace of God. If we can be justified through the law, then Christ's death was needless. . . .

Here is some bold lettering for you, written in my own hand. Who are they, these people who insist on your being circumcised? They are men, all of them, who are determined to keep up outward appearances, so that the cross of Christ may not bring persecution on them. Why, they do not even observe the law, although they adopt circumcision; they are for having you circumcised, so as to make a display of your outward conformity. God forbid that I should make a display of anything, except the cross of our Lord Jesus Christ, through which the world stands crucified to me, and I to the world. Circumcision means nothing, the want of it means nothing; when a man is in

Christ Jesus, there has been a new creation. Peace and pardon to all those who follow this rule, to God's true Israel. Spare me, all of you, any further anxieties; already I bear the scars of the Lord Jesus printed on my body.

Brethren, the grace of our Lord Jesus Christ be with your spirit. Amen. (Gal. 1. 11-2. 21; 6. 11-18.)

Since we live by the spirit, let the spirit be our rule of life; we must not indulge vain ambitions, envying one another and provoking one another to envy. (Gal. 5. 25-6.)

The spirit which should govern the exercise of zeal

Brethren, if a man is found guilty of some fault, you, who are spiritually minded, ought to shew a spirit of gentleness in correcting him. Have an eye upon thyself; thou too wilt perhaps encounter temptation. Bear the burden of one another's failings; then you will be fulfilling the law of Christ. The man who thinks he is of some worth, when in truth he is worth nothing at all, is merely deluding himself. Everyone should examine his own conscience; then he will be able to take the measure of his own worth; no need to compare himself with others. Each of us, then, will have his own load to carry.

Your teachers are to have a share in all that their disciples have to bestow. Make no mistake about it; you cannot cheat God. A man will reap what he sows; if nature is his seed-ground, nature will give him a perishable harvest, if his seed-ground is the spirit, it will give him a harvest of eternal life. Let us not be discouraged, then, over our acts of charity; we shall reap when the time comes, if we persevere in them. Let us practise generosity to all, while the opportunity is ours; and above all, to those who are of one family with us in the faith. (Gal. 6. 1-10.)

THE PRAYER OF THE FIRST CHRISTIANS

Prayers in the Acts of the Apostles

Ruler of all, thou art the maker of heaven and earth and the sea, and all that is in them. Thou has said by thy Holy Spirit, by the lips of thy servant David, our father,
What means this turmoil among the nations;
Why do the peoples cherish vain dreams?
See how the kings of the earth stand in array,
How its rulers make common cause,
Against the Lord and his Christ.
True enough, in this city of ours, Herod and Pontius Pilate, with the Gentiles and the people of Israel to aid them, made common cause against thy holy servant Jesus, so accomplishing all that thy power and wisdom had decreed. Look down upon their threats, Lord, now as of old; enable thy servants to preach thy word confidently, by stretching out thy hand to heal; and let signs and miracles be performed in the name of Jesus, thy holy Son. (Acts 4. 24-30.)

Letter to the Romans: Hymn to the divine wisdom

How deep is the mine of God's wisdom, of his knowledge; how inscrutable are his judgements, how undiscoverable are his ways! Who has ever understood the Lord's thoughts, or been his counsellor? Who ever was the first to give, and so earned his favours? All things find in him their origin, their impulse, the centre of their being; to him be glory throughout all ages, Amen. (Romans 11. 33-6.)

Prayer for the brethren

May God, the author of all endurance and all encouragement, enable you to be all of one mind according to the mind of Christ Jesus, so that you may all have but one heart and one mouth to glorify God, the Father of our Lord Jesus Christ. (Romans 15. 5,6.)

May God, the author of our hope, fill you with all joy and peace in your believing; so that you may have hope in abundance, through the power of the Holy Spirit. (Romans 15. 13.)

May God, the author of peace, be with you all, Amen. (Romans 15. 33.)

So God, who is the author of peace, will crush Satan under your feet before long. May the grace of our Lord Jesus Christ be with you. (Romans 16. 20.)

Doxology

There is one who is able to set your feet firmly in the path of that gospel which I preach, when I herald Jesus Christ; a gospel which reveals the mystery, hidden from us through countless ages, but now made plain, through what the prophets have written; now published, at the eternal God's command, to all the nations, so as to win the homage of their faith. To him, to God who alone is wise, glory be given from age to age, through Jesus Christ, Amen. (Romans 16. 25-7.)

Letter to the Corinthians: Thanksgiving

Grace and peace be yours from God, who is our Father, and from the Lord Jesus Christ. I give thanks to my God continually in your name for that grace of God which has been bestowed upon you in Jesus Christ; that you have become rich, through him, in every way, in eloquence and in knowledge of every sort; so fully has the message of Christ established itself among you. And now there is no gift in which you are still lacking; you have only to look forward to the revealing of our Lord Jesus Christ. He will strengthen your resolution to the last, so that no charge will lie against you on the day when our Lord Jesus Christ comes. The God, who has called you into the fellowship of his Son, Jesus Christ our Lord, is faithful to his promise. (1 Cor. 1. 3-9.)

A hymn to charity

I may speak with every tongue that men and angels use; yet, if I lack charity, I am no better than echoing bronze, or the clash of cymbals. I may have powers of prophecy, no secret hidden from me, no knowledge too deep for me; I may have utter faith, so that I can move mountains; yet if I lack charity, I count for nothing. I may give away all that I have, to feed the poor; I may give myself up to be burnt at the stake; if I lack charity, it goes for nothing.

Charity is patient, is kind; charity feels no envy; charity is never perverse or proud, never insolent; does not claim its rights, cannot be provoked, does not brood over an injury; takes no pleasure in wrong-doing, but rejoices at the victory of the truth; sustains, believes, hopes, endures, to the last.

The time will come when we shall outgrow prophecy, when speaking with tongues will come to an end, when knowledge will be swept away; we shall never have finished with charity.

Our knowledge, our prophecy, are only glimpses of the truth; and these glimpses will be swept away when the time of fulfilment comes. (Just so, when I was a child, I talked like a child, I had the intelligence, the thoughts of a child; since I became a man, I have outgrown childish ways.)

At present, we are looking at a confused reflection in a mirror; then, we shall see face to face; now, I have only glimpses of knowledge; then, I shall recognize God as he has recognized me. Meanwhile, faith, hope and charity

persist, all three; but the greatest of them all is charity.
(1 Cor. 13.)

Blessing

Grace and peace be yours from God, our Father, and
from the Lord Jesus Christ.

Blessed be the God and Father of our Lord Jesus
Christ, the merciful Father, the God who gives all encouragement. He it is who comforts us in all our trials;
and it is this encouragement we ourselves receive from
God which enables us to comfort others, whenever they
have trials of their own. (2 Cor. 1. 2-4.)

Letter to the Ephesians: Blessing

Blessed be that God, that Father of our Lord Jesus
Christ, who has blessed us, in Christ, with every spiritual
blessing, higher than heaven itself.

He has chosen us out, in Christ, before the foundation
of the world, to be saints, to be blameless in his sight, for
love of him; marking us out beforehand (so his will
decreed) to be his adopted children through Jesus Christ.
Thus he would manifest the splendour of his grace by
which he has taken us into his favour in the person of his
beloved Son.

It is in him and through his blood that we enjoy redemption, the forgiveness of our sins. So rich is God's
grace, that has overflowed upon us in a full stream of
wisdom and discernment, to make known to us the hidden purpose of his will.

It was his loving design, centred in Christ, to give
history its fulfilment by resuming everything in him, all
that is in heaven, all that is on earth, summed up in him.

In him it was our lot to be called, singled out beforehand to suit his purpose (for it is he who is at work
everywhere, carrying out the designs of his will); we were

to manifest his glory, we who were the first to set our hope in Christ; in him you too were called, when you listened to the preaching of the truth, that gospel which is your salvation. In him you too learned to believe, and had the seal set on your faith by the promised gift of the Holy Spirit; a pledge of the inheritance which is ours, to redeem it for us and bring us into possession of it, and so manifest God's glory.

Well then, I too play my part; I have been told of your faith in the Lord Jesus, of the love you shew towards all the saints, and I never cease to offer thanks on your behalf, or to remember you in my prayers. So may he who is the God of our Lord Jesus Christ, the Father to whom glory belongs, grant you a spirit of wisdom and insight, to give you fuller knowledge of himself. May your inward eye be enlightened, so that you may understand to what hopes he has called you, how rich in glory is that inheritance of his found among the saints, what surpassing virtue there is in his dealings with us, who believe. (Ephes. 1. 3-19.)

Prayer

I fall on my knees to the Father of our Lord Jesus Christ, that Father from whom all fatherhood in heaven and on earth takes its title. May he, out of the rich treasury of his glory, strengthen you through his Spirit with a power that reaches your innermost being. May Christ find a dwelling-place, through faith, in your hearts; may your lives be rooted in love, founded on love. May you and all the saints be enabled to measure, in all its breadth and length and height and depth, the love of Christ, to know what passes knowledge. May you be filled with all the completion God has to give.

He whose power is at work in us is powerful enough, and more than powerful enough, to carry out his purpose beyond all our hopes and dreams; may he be glorified in the Church, and in Christ Jesus, to the last generation of eternity. Amen. (Ephes. 3. 14-21.)

Letter to the Philippians: Thanksgiving

I give thanks to my God for all my memories of you, happy at all times in all the prayer I offer for all of you; so full a part have you taken in the work of Christ's gospel, from the day when it first reached you till now. Nor am I less confident, that he who has inspired this generosity in you will bring it to perfection, ready for the day when Jesus Christ comes.

It is only fitting that I should entertain such hopes for you; you who are close to my heart, and I know that you all share my happiness in being a prisoner, and being able to defend and assert the truth of the gospel. God knows how I long for you all, with the tenderness of Jesus Christ himself.

And this is my prayer for you; may your love grow richer and richer yet, in the fulness of its knowledge and the depth of its perception, so that you may learn to prize what is of value; may nothing cloud your consciences or hinder your progress till the day when Christ comes; may you reap, through Jesus Christ, the full harvest of your justification to God's glory and praise. (Phil. 1. 3-11.)

Letter to the Colossians: Prayer

So, ever since the news reached us, we have been praying for you in return, unceasingly. Our prayer is, that you may be filled with that closer knowledge of God's will which brings all wisdom and all spiritual insight with it. May you live as befits his servants, waiting continually on his pleasure; may the closer knowledge of God bring you fruitfulness and growth in all good. May you be inspired, as his glorious power can inspire you, with full strength to be patient and to endure; to endure joyfully, thanking God our Father for making us fit to share the light which saints inherit, for rescuing us from the power of darkness, and transferring us to the kingdom of his beloved Son, [in whom] we have the redemption that sets us free from our sins. (Col. 1. 9-14.)

Hymns or lyrical chants, recorded by St Paul

Awake, thou that sleepest, and arise from the dead, and Christ shall give thee light. (Ephes. 5. 14.)

Honour and glory through endless ages to the king of all the ages, the immortal, the invisible, who alone is God, Amen. (1 Tim. 1. 17.)[1]

No question of it, it is a great mystery we worship. Revelation made in human nature, justification won in the realm of the Spirits; a vision seen by angels, a mystery preached to the Gentiles; Christ in this world, accepted by faith, Christ, on high, taken up into glory. (1 Tim. 3. 16.)

The blessed God who alone enjoys dominion; he is King of kings, and Lord of lords; to him alone immortality belongs, his dwelling is in unapproachable light; no human eye has seen or can ever see him; to him be glory and everlasting empire, Amen. (1 Tim. 6. 15-16.)

We are to share his life, because we have shared his death; if we endure, we shall reign with him, if we disown him, he in his turn will disown us. If we play him false, he remains true to his word; he cannot disown himself. (2 Tim. 2. 11-13.)

That is why, when we give glory to God, it is through him that we say our Amen. (2 Cor. 1. 20.)

---

[1] The Church has included this magnificent doxology in her morning prayer, the Hour of Prime.

St Jude's letter

There is one who can keep you clear of fault, and enable you to stand in the presence of his glory, triumphant and unreproved, . . . to him, who alone is God, who gives us salvation through Jesus Christ our Lord, glory and majesty and power and domination are due, before time was, and now, and for all ages, Amen. (Jude 24,25.)

The hymns of the Apocalypse: Doxologies

He has proved his love for us, by washing us clean from our sins in his own blood, and made us a royal race of priests, to serve God, his Father; glory and power be his through endless ages, Amen.

Holy, holy, holy is the Lord God, the Almighty, who ever was, and is, and is still to come. (Apoc. 1. 5-6; 4. 8.)

Hymns to the Lamb

Thou, our Lord God, claimest as thy due glory and honour and power; by thee all things were created; nothing ever was, nothing was ever created, but in obedience to thy will. (Apoc. 4. 11.)

Thou, Lord, art worthy to take up the book and break the seals that are on it. Thou wast slain in sacrifice; out of every tribe, every language, every people, every nation thou hast ransomed us with thy blood and given us to God. Thou hast made us a royal race of priests, to serve God; we shall reign as kings over the earth. (Apoc. 5. 9-10.)

Power and Godhead, wisdom and strength, honour and glory and blessing are his by right, the Lamb that was slain. (Apoc. 5. 12.)

Blessing and honour and glory and power, through endless ages, to him who sits on the throne, and to the Lamb.
Amen. (Apoc. 5. 13.)

The hymn of the Lamb

Lord God Almighty, the deeds thou doest are great and
wonderful; King of all the ages, thy ways are just and
true. Lord, who alone art holy, who shall refuse reverence
and glory to thy name? All the nations shall come and fall
down before thee, now that thy just retribution has been
made known. (Apoc. 15. 3-4.)

Hymn of triumph

Alleluia!

Salvation and glory and power belong to our God; his
sentence is ever true and just, and now he has given
sentence against the great harlot, who poisoned the earth
with her harlot's ways; now he has called her to account
for the blood of his servants.

Alleluia! The smoke of her burning goes up everlast-
ingly.

Amen. Alleluia!

Praise our God, all you that are his servants, and all
you that fear him, little and great alike.

Alleluia! the Lord our God, the Almighty, has claimed
his kingdom; let us rejoice and triumph and give him the
praise; the time has come for the wedding-feast of the
Lamb. His bride has clothed herself in readiness for it;
hers it is to wear linen of shining white. (Apoc. 19.
1-2,3,4,5,6-8.)

Prayer of expectation

Come! Come!

Indeed I am coming soon.

Be it so, then; come, Lord Jesus.

May the grace of our Lord Jesus Christ be with you all.
Amen. (Apoc. 22. 17,20-1.)

DEATH AMONG THE FIRST CHRISTIANS

St Stephen's preaching and martyrdom

Stephen, full of grace and power, performed great miracles and signs among the people. There were those who
came forward to debate with him, some of the synagogue
of the Freedmen (as it is called), and of the Cyreneans
and Alexandrians, and of those who came from Cilicia
and Asia; but they were no match for Stephen's wisdom,
and for the Spirit which then gave utterance. Thereupon
they employed agents to say they had heard him speaking
blasphemously of Moses, and of God. Having thus roused
the feelings of the people, and of the elders and scribes,
they set upon him and carried him off, and so brought
him before the Council. There they put forward false witnesses, who declared, This man is never tired of uttering
insults against the holy place, and the law. We have heard
him say that the Nazarene, Jesus, will destroy this place,
and will alter the traditions which Moses handed down to
us. And all those who sat there in the Council fastened
their eyes on him, and saw his face looking like the face
of an angel.

Then the high priest asked, Are these charges true?
And he answered, Brethren and fathers, listen to me.
When the God of glory appeared to our father Abraham,
it was while he was still in Mesopotamia, before he took
up his dwelling in Charan. Leave thy country, he said, and
thy kindred, and come to the land to which I direct thee.
So it was that he left the country of the Chaldaeans, and
lived in Charan; it was only after his father's death that
he was bidden to remove thence into this land where you
now dwell. There, God gave him no inheritance, not so

much as a foot's space; he only promised the possession
of it to him and to his posterity after him, although at this
time he had no child. And this is what God told him, that
his descendants would live as strangers in a foreign land,
where they would be enslaved and ill-used for four hundred years. But I will pass judgement, the Lord said, on
the nation which enslaves them; and at last they will
escape, and settle down to worship me here. Then he
made a covenant with Abraham, the covenant that ordained circumcision. So it was that he became the father
of Isaac, whom he circumcised seven days afterwards,
and Isaac of Jacob, and Jacob of the twelve patriarchs.

The patriarchs, out of jealousy, sold Joseph as a slave,
to be taken to Egypt. In Egypt, God was with him; he
rescued him from all his afflictions, and won him favour
and a name for wisdom with Pharao, king of Egypt, who
made him ruler over Egypt and over all the royal household. And now a famine came upon all Egypt and Ca-
naan, cruelly afflicting them, till our fathers could procure
no food. So Jacob, hearing that there was corn in Egypt,
sent out our fathers on their first journey; and on their
second journey Joseph made himself known to them, and
Pharao learned about Joseph's kindred. Then Joseph sent
for his father Jacob, and for his family, seventy-five souls
in all; and Jacob went down into Egypt, where he and our
fathers died. They were removed afterwards to Sichem;
and it was in the grave which Abraham had bought for a
sum of money from the sons of Hemor, the man of
Sichem, that they were buried.

And when the time drew near for the fulfilment of the
promise which God had made to Abraham, the people
had increased and multiplied in Egypt. And now a new
king arose in Egypt, one who knew nothing of Joseph;
this king dealt treacherously with our race, using them so
ill that they exposed their children, instead of rearing

them. It was at this time that Moses was born, and, finding favour with God, was brought up in his father's house for three months; then, when he had been exposed, he was rescued by Pharao's daughter, who adopted him as her son. Thus Moses was well trained in all the learning of the Egyptians; he was vigorous, too, in speech and in act. And now, when he had reached forty years of age, it came into his mind to visit his brethren, the children of Israel. When he saw one of them being unjustly used, he came to the rescue and avenged the man who was wronged, by killing the Egyptian. He expected them to understand, but they could not understand, that he was the means by which God was to bring them deliverance. Next day, he came in sight when two of them were quarreling, and tried to restore peace between them; Sirs, he said, you are brethren; why do you inflict injury on one another? Whereupon the man who was doing his neighbour a wrong thrust him aside, asking, Who made thee a ruler and judge over us? Art thou ready to kill me, as thou didst kill the Egyptian yesterday? And at that Moses fled, and lived as an exile in the land of Madian; it was there that two sons were born to him.

Forty years later, a vision came to him in the wilderness of mount Sinai; a bush had caught fire; and an angel was standing among the flames. Moses saw it, and was astonished at the sight; and as he drew near to look, the voice of the Lord came to him. I am the God of thy fathers, of Abraham, of Isaac, and Jacob. And Moses did not dare to look close; fear made him tremble. Then the Lord said to him, Take the shoes off thy feet; the place on which thou standest is holy ground. The affliction of my people in Egypt is before my eyes continually; I have heard their lamenting, and have come down to deliver them. Come now, I have an errand for thee in Egypt. It was this same Moses, the man whom they had disowned, and asked him, Who made thee a ruler and a judge over us? that God sent to be their ruler and deliverer, helped by the angel whom he saw there at the bush. He it was who led them out, performing wonders and signs in Egypt, and at the Red Sea, and in the wilderness, over a space of forty years.

It was this Moses who said to the children of Israel, The Lord your God will raise up for you a prophet like myself, from among your own brethren; to him you must listen. He it was who took part with the angel that spoke to him on Mount Sinai, and with our fathers, at the meeting in the desert. There he received words of life to hand on to us; and yet our fathers would not give him obedience. They disowned him; they turned their thoughts towards Egypt, and said to Aaron, Make us gods, to lead our march; as for this Moses, who brought us out of the land of Egypt, there is no saying what has become of him. So they fashioned a calf at this time, making offerings to an idol, and keeping holiday over the works of their own hands. Whereupon God turned away from them, and gave them over to the worship of all the host of heaven; so it is written in the book of the prophets, Is it true that you brought me victims and sacrifices, you sons of Israel, for forty years in the wilderness? You carried about the tent of Moloch, and the star of your god Rempham, and worshipped them, images of your own fashioning. And now I will send you into exile on the further side of Babylon.

In the wilderness, our fathers had the tabernacle with them, to remind them of God's covenant; he who spoke to Moses bade them fashion it after the model which he had shown him. And when God dispossessed the Gentiles, to make room for our fathers' coming, our fathers under Josue brought this tabernacle, as an heirloom, into the land which they had conquered. So it was until the time of

David. David, who had won favour in God's sight, longed to devise a resting-place for the God of Israel, but in the end it was Solomon who built the house for him. Yet we are not to think that the Most High dwells in temples made by men's hands; the prophet says; Heaven is my throne, and earth is the footstool under my feet. What home will you build for me, says the Lord, what place can be my resting-place? Was it not my hands that made all this?

Stiff-necked race, your heart and ears still uncircumcised, you are for ever resisting the Holy Spirit, just as your fathers did. There was not one of the prophets they did not persecute; it was death to foretell the coming of that just man, whom you in these times have betrayed and murdered; you, who received the law dictated by angels, and did not keep it.

At hearing this, they were cut to the heart, and began to gnash their teeth at him. But he, full of the Holy Spirit, fastened his eyes on heaven, and saw there the glory of God, and Jesus standing at God's right hand; I see heaven opening, he said, and the Son of Man standing at the right hand of God. Then they cried aloud, and put their fingers into their ears; with one accord they fell upon him, thrust him out of the city, and stoned him. And the witnesses put down their clothes at the feet of a young man named Saul. Thus they stoned Stephen; he, meanwhile, was praying; Lord Jesus, he said, receive my spirit; and then, kneeling down, he cried aloud, Lord, do not count this sin against them. And with that, he fell asleep in the Lord.

Saul was one of those who gave their voices for his his murder.

The church in Jerusalem was much persecuted at this time, and all except the apostles were scattered about

over the countryside of Judaea and Samaria. Stephen was
buried by devout men, who mourned greatly over him.
Saul, meanwhile, was making havoc of the church; he
made his way into house after house, carrying men and
women off and committing them to prison. (Acts 6. 8-
8. 3.)

The martyrdom of James and the miraculous
deliverance of Peter

Herod exerted his authority to persecute some of those
who belonged to the Church. James, the brother of John,
he beheaded, and then, finding that this was acceptable
to the Jews, he went further, and laid hands on Peter
too. It was the time of unleavened bread; and he imprisoned Peter, after arresting him, with a guard of four
soldiers, relieved four times a day; when paschaltime was
over, he would bring him out in the presence of the people. Peter, then, was well guarded in prison, but there
was a continual stream of prayer going up to God from
the church on his behalf. And now the day was coming
when Herod was to bring him out; that night, Peter was
sleeping with two chains on him, between two soldiers,
and there were warders at the door guarding his prison.
Suddenly an angel of the Lord stood over him, and a light
shone in his cell. He smote Peter on the side, to rouse
him; Quick, he said rise up; and thereupon the chains
fell from his hands. Then the angel said to him, Gird
thyself up, and put on thy shoes; and, when he had done
this, Throw thy cloak over thee, and follow me. So he
followed him out, unaware that what the angel had done
for him was true; he thought he was seeing a vision. Thus
they passed one party of guards, then a second, and
reached the iron gate which leads out into the city; this
opened for them of its own accord. They came out, and

as soon as they had passed on up one street, the angel left him.

At this, Peter came to himself. Now I can tell for certain, he said, that the Lord has sent his angel, to deliver me out of Herod's hands, and from all that the people of the Jews hoped to see. After some thought, he made for the house belonging to Mary the mother of John, also called Mark. Here many had gathered for prayer; a girl named Rhoda came to answer, when he knocked at the porch door, and she, recognizing Peter's voice, was too overjoyed to open the gate for him; she ran in, and told them that Peter was standing at the gate. Thou art mad, they told her, but she still insisted that it was so; and then they said, It must be his guardian angel. Meanwhile, Peter went on knocking; so they opened, and found him there, and stood astonished. Calling for silence by a gesture of his hand, he told them how the Lord had delivered him from prison; Give news of this, he said, to James and the rest of the brethren. And so he left them, and went elsewhere.

When day broke, there was a great to-do among the soldiers, to know what had become of Peter. Herod, after searching for him without avail, questioned the warders and had them punished. Then he went down from Judaea to Caesarea, and spent his time there. He was much out of humour with the people of Tyre and Sidon; and these, since their country depended on the king's country for its supplies, waited upon him by common consent, and tried (by winning over Blastus, the royal chamberlain) to make their peace. So, on an appointed day, Herod put on his royal finery and sat down on a raised dais to harangue them; whereupon the people cried out in applause, It is no man, it is a god that speaks. And immediately the angel of the Lord smote him, for not referring the glory to God; and he was eaten up by worms, and so died.

And still the word of God grew strong and spread wide. Barnabas and Saul returned from Jerusalem, their mission of relief fulfilled, and took John, also called Mark, in their company. (Acts 12. 1-25.)

CHAPTER II

FROM THE FIRST ENCOUNTERS WITH THE PAGAN EMPIRE TO THE PEACE UNDER COMMODUS

The new society we find in the Acts and the Epistles is the primitive community, presenting a spectacle hitherto unknown to the world: an integral brotherhood. The first Christians, as we have seen, lived in a close unity of spirit with one another, always dwelling on the thought of their Lord's return, which they expected at the end of the world—but could that be long delayed?—and perpetuating his memory by the repetition of the sacred rite instituted by him before his death, the rite which revived his real presence in their midst through the life-giving power of the renewal of his own words: "This is my Body. This is my Blood. Do this, whenever you drink it, for a commemoration of me." But after these words his last command had been that of mutual love: ". . . you are to love one another; that your love for one another is to be like the love I have borne you," so as to reproduce in them the very union of the divine Persons: "Father . . . that they should all be one, as we are one," and they tried to take his words literally. They pooled all their goods, the rich selling theirs in order to give the price to the poor. It was a generous sacrifice, reasonable enough when an early end to the world was expected, but imprudent if earthly life was to be prolonged. Soon, in fact, it made the Jerusalem community a charge on the others, who kept only the spirit of this charity, without copying its form.

But this was indeed the spirit everywhere, and the verse in the Acts (4. 32) which says: "None of them called any of his possessions his own, everything was shared in common," accurately describes, at least in the disposition it reveals, the spirit of all the Christians of those early days. The Church flourished in an atmosphere of love and holiness. She allowed no respect of persons: as St Paul says, there is now neither Greek nor Jew, neither slave nor free. Such words did not legally abolish slavery, but they were enough to effect a radical transformation of it, actually inherent as it was in ancient society, but clearly incompatible in principle with the moral demands of Christianity. So we are not surprised to see St Paul again, in his letter to Philemon, intervening with the calm assurance of a man who is sure of being obeyed, to obtain pardon for Onesimus, a slave who had run away from his master's house, and not hesitating to write: "counting on thy obedience" to receive Onesimus back "as a well loved brother."

This mutual love was soon the sign by which the Christians were recognized. "See how they love one another," the pagans said about them.

This brotherliness of the early communities was found even in their organization: there was nothing domineering in their authority. Those in command were the "servants" of those they had to lead. But of course there had to be men who, because they were the men chosen by Christ, or had been appointed by them in turn, instructed their brethren and gave them rules of conduct. St Clement, the third successor of St Peter, firmly rebuked some unruly brethren. An organization, hierarchical because the original authority came from none other than the Lord, existed from the beginning: the *presbyterium,* the college of Presbyters or Elders, having at its head one to whom, after some time, was reserved the title of bishop. In some communities, like Antioch, the bishop embodied all authority in himself, while in others the episcopate was not immediately monarchical but remained for some time collegiate.

But everywhere the Christian community of each town —for early Christianity was essentially a religion of the towns—formed a single body, the *universitas* of the Christians of that town. Through the whole body, as through every other reached by the gospel message, circulated the same life, proceeding wholly from the love of Christ who had bidden his disciples to be but one, and maintained in being by the ever-renewed commemoration of the gift he had made of himself, at the Last Supper before his death, and in his death itself, for these two are inseparable. This was the essential "sacrament" of the first Christians, source of grace, the Eucharist. But it was preceded by another which brought them into the Church, the baptism of water, perfected by the gift of the Spirit, confirming them in the faith.

This eucharistic liturgy, accompanied by prayers and chants, hymns and canticles, and supplemented by private prayers at certain times of day, though without any rigidity or constraint, constituted at first the whole of Christian worship. It was substantially the same wherever the gospel had been preached and received, whether in Rome or in other places in the West where it had been carried in the first century: at Corinth or Athens, at Alexandria or Antioch, on the banks of the Euphrates or beyond. Everywhere a disciple of Jesus going from one place to another found himself at home. Everywhere he found the same faith, the same prayer, the same life-blood circulating in the current of the same charity. This is attested by the letters of the apostles and equally, in the next generation, by a letter like that of St Clement to the Church of Corinth in a time of disturbance; a letter inspired with one single love, anxious both to recall the wandering to the right path and to safeguard the unity threatened by dissensions. Underlying this famous letter is brotherly solicitude on the part of the Church of Rome for a Church bound to it by ties of ancient and particular friendship, but also awareness of being responsible for an authority inherited from Peter, and therefore obliged to recall Christians, whether individuals or groups, to their duty. But even in correction and reproof the words of this authority correspond to the general feeling: the veneration which always surrounded this *Epistula Clementis*, ranking it almost with the canonical Epistles, is eloquent proof of that. Thus from one end to the other of the young Christian world there was proof of a universal consensus, a brotherly solidarity whose substantial bond was Christ himself.

What were the dimensions of the Christian world at the end of its first century? If it was not yet co-extensive with the Roman Empire, it had penetrated or at least touched practically all its provinces, and at some points crossed its frontiers. Syria, with Palestine, its own cradle, Asia Minor, Macedonia and Greece with the Aegean Isles, Rome and southern Italy had not only heard the good news proclaimed but responded in already large numbers. Evidence is not lacking that at this time there were Christian centres in Roman Africa, Spain, southern Gaul and, quite certainly, in Egypt, while beyond the Euphrates and even the Tigris, in Rome's rival empire of Persia, the seed sown had begun to bear fruit.

The proportion of the Christian population, nowhere large, must of course have varied greatly. It seems to have been strongest in Asia Minor, while we can scarcely do more than guess the growth of certain seeds in Gaul or Spain. But the Church had taken spiritual possession of the Empire's capital: the apostles Peter and Paul had sealed their presence in the heart of the Roman world with their blood. From this time forward it is impossible to separate Rome from the kingdom of Christ.

Rome, however, soon tried to destroy it. Not that Rome was violently hostile in principle to the introduction of new religions: rather, she even welcomed them, but only on condition that they were integrated into her own, or at least compromised with it. It was therefore all too clear that the tradition of pagan Rome and the religion of Christ were incompatible in principle. Incompatibilities of doctrine, however, do not always exclude the possibility of coexistence, and in spite of incidents like those which had brought Paul to the capital as a prisoner, though not under sentence, the free propagation of Christianity might probably have gone on for some time, but for one tragic event.

The great fire of Rome in 64, for which the almost unanimous and perhaps well-informed opinion of Rome blamed the emperor Nero, provoked the terrible reaction on his part which has never been forgotten. The Christian community of Rome was decimated with appalling tortures, including its leaders Peter and Paul, though there is some question as to the date of their martyrdoms, which may not have been simultaneous. But a lasting ban followed.

There is no proof, though perhaps there are some signs,

that the persecution raged outside Rome, but from this day onwards Christianity was legally proscribed: the very name of Christian, and not merely such crimes as might be imputed to Christians, was condemned. "It is not lawful for Christians to exist": these words sum up the legislation directed against Christianity.

This does not mean that Christianity now suffered unceasing persecution. Nearly half a century went by before it really flared up again under the emperor Trajan, although in the interval, under Domitian, some Christians of the Roman aristocracy among whom the faith had spread, even close to the throne, had been suspected, and some, apparently, condemned. But when conversions had multiplied in certain provinces, such as Bithynia on the shores of the Black Sea, the Roman magistrates took alarm and executions took place. The governor of the province, none other than the writer, Pliny the Younger, was informed and, puzzled at the situation now revealed and the extent of the penalties apparently involved, he referred the problem to Trajan, whose reply was to have the force of law for nearly two hundred years.

It was a strange reply, making Christianity a capital offence when admitted, but one which the authorities were not to prosecute on their own initiative. The Christian who was denounced and admitted his faith was to be condemned for it alone, but if he denied it he was acquitted. This denial was what the authorities often did their utmost to obtain. The object of the persecutions was henceforth not so much to punish a crime as to procure its disavowal. But except in some periods of weakness or panic the Christians, with marvellous courage, refused for two centuries to give this disavowal to the Roman power, when summoned to make it. It is true that these demands were only issued at intervals: the persecution was intermittent in time and sporadic in the area of the Roman world. But for two centuries the threat never ceased to hang over the heads of those who, if it fell, would be its victims, but often joyful victims, longing for that martyrdom which loomed so large in their thoughts.

Such a one was St Ignatius, bishop of Antioch, one of the most illustrious witnesses of Christ in the post-apostolic generation, who when being taken to Rome to be tortured, looked forward impatiently to being "ground by the teeth of the beasts." A little earlier, there was the aged bishop of Jerusalem, Simeon, the last of those near kinsmen of Jesus who were called "the Lord's brethren." Crucified at the age of over a hundred and twenty, his courage astonished the governor himself.

After the persecution under Trajan there was again a period of comparative peace. The Christians were not yet numerous enough to provoke widespread hostile reactions, and the emperors of the Antonine dynasty had no liking for unnecessary severity. They even tended to discourage denunciations. These still occurred, however, and the Stoic philosopher Epictetus knew some martyrs. But under Marcus Aurelius there was an eruption in many provinces and Christian blood was again shed, thereby eventually revealing to posterity (ignorant of the details of the progress of the Gospel), that its conquering march had never been halted. In about a hundred years after the death of the apostles Peter and Paul it had reached not only a great part of the east but most of the important cities of the west; northern Italy with its metropolitan cities, Milan, Ravenna and Aquileia, south-east Gaul with Lyons, northern Africa and most probably Spain also, though precise proofs of this are lacking.

But because these converted Romans worshipped one invisible God, because they did not take part in the sacrifices offered to the traditional deities of Rome, Greece or the east, because they were distinguished from others by the practice of a stricter morality, they were all signs of contradiction. If their love of their neighbours was generous enough to excite admiration, it did not avail to dispel suspicions which grew to hate. Denunciations abounded and hostile movements increased, stimulated by the disasters which began to afflict the empire in the time of Marcus Aurelius, and so did the number of Christians called on to confess their faith.

A great bishop, St Polycarp of Smyrna—who still belongs, so to speak, to the apostolic generation since in his youth he had seen St John, the author of a letter to the Church of Philippi in Macedonia, a letter almost as famous as those of St Ignatius—perished in his episcopal city, the victim of a sudden outbreak of popular hatred. Throughout the neighbouring regions Christians were arrested and condemned. The bishop of Athens and other Christians were martyred, and so was the philosopher-apologist Justin in Rome, with several others of the faithful. Then in Gaul persecution broke out violently at Lyons, where the young but already very vigorous Church was ruled by its founder-bishop Pothinus, like other clerics and laity a native of Asia Minor. These martyrs of Lyons have told their own story in a document which will always be famous, the letter of the Church of Lyons to the Churches of Asia and Phrygia. It is one of the noblest relics of Christian antiquity, telling in the simplest manner a tale of atrocious sufferings but still breathing the ardour of the contest waged for the love of Christ, and showing how these men, faced with the threat of the direst penalties, could still care for everything which concerned the universal Church of their time, encouraging one another, full of brotherly pity for some who had weakened, then rejoicing to see them rally and rejoin them in suffering and death. About fifty perished, both Easterns and Gauls. The old bishop succumbed in prison, while

Blandina, a young slave-girl hardly more than a child, was put to every kind of torture, till the very pagans exclaimed that they had never seen a woman endure so many and cruel torments.

At the beginning of the reign of Marcus Aurelius' successor Commodus there were more martyrs. In Africa, where they had not been known before, twelve Christians of the little town of Scillium in Numidia, known as the Scillitan Martyrs, were condemned to death by the sword in 180. In Asia Minor, where again, in an atmosphere of heated passions, denunciations against the Christians did not slacken, Arrius Antoninus, a proconsul related to the imperial family, seemed to encourage them, to such an extent that he provoked an unexpected and disconcerting reaction from the Christians: in a town where he was holding his assizes the Christians appeared in a body at his tribunal, demanding to be dealt with. Alarmed at their large numbers, he had some of them arrested and sent the others away, exclaiming: "Wretched men, if you want to die, have you not enough ropes and precipices?" Finally Rome had an illustrious martyr, Apollonius, who read out, in a meeting of the Senate, an apology for the Christian religion. The prefect of the praetorium, representing the emperor, did all he could to obtain at least an apparent abjuration, which would have saved him, but in vain, and he was beheaded in accordance with the existing laws.

The political atmosphere, however, was changing. Commodus had a favourite called Marcia, who had entered the palace as a slave and ended by becoming his wife, though he did not give her the imperial title. Now Marcia was a Christian, by faith if not by baptism. Although her life had not always been in conformity with the standards of the Gospel, she was no doubt a woman of good will, who did all she could to mitigate the lot of her brethren. She obtained the pardon of several Christians sentenced to the legally capital punishment of forced labour in the mines among whom was a future pope, the freedman Callistus, and they were released without even a feigned denial of their faith being required. An unexpected *modus vivendi* seems then to have been established between the Church and the Empire, and another Christian freedman, Proxenes, is known to have been the emperor's chamberlain. It was a providential relaxation of those rigid principles from which none of the Antonines, from Trajan to Marcus Aurelius, had felt free to deviate.

The growth in the number of the faithful, as shown by the very multitude of previous condemnations, their penetration into the imperial palace itself, the ease with which the provincial authorities adapted themselves to the new line of action, all surely signified that the old system, faced with an irresistible movement, would not work. The only bad emperor of the second century, who has earned the reputation of being the most indifferent to his duties as a ruler, by a paradox which was only apparent and certainly unsuspected by himself, happened to be more far-seeing than his conscientious predecessors when he took the first measure of benevolence of the Roman power towards the Church. After this, for severity to be resumed, at least on any large scale and for any time, the emperors were obliged to take fresh measures, though without repealing the former laws.

CONTEMPORARY DOCUMENTS

PRAYERS OF SECOND-CENTURY CHRISTIANS

A Universal Prayer

May the Creator of the Universe preserve undiminished on the earth the determined number of his elect, through his beloved Servant, Jesus Christ. Through him he has called us out of darkness into light, from ignorance to the knowledge of the glory of thy name. We put our trust in thee, from whom every creature comes forth. Thou hast opened the eyes of our hearts, that we may know thee, who alone art all-High, in the highest, the Holy, reposing among the holy.

Thou humblest the insolence of the proud, thou destroyest the designs of the nations, thou exaltest the lowly and humblest the lofty; thou makest rich and makest poor, thou takest away life and givest it, thou alone art benefactor of spirits and the God of all flesh; thou gazest upon the depths, thou beholdest men's works, O Succour in danger, saviour in despair! Thou multipliest the nations of the earth, and out of them all thou hast chosen those who love thee, through Jesus Christ thy Servant, through whom thou hast taught them, hallowed them, honoured them.

We beseech thee, Master, to be our support and our defender. Save the oppressed, have pity on the lowly, raise up the fallen, show thyself to those in need, heal the sick, bring back those of thy people who have strayed, feed the hungry, free the prisoners, set the weak upon their feet, comfort the fainthearted, and let all the nations know that thou only art God, that Jesus Christ is thy Servant, that we are thy people and the sheep of thy fold.

By thy works thou hast made known the eternal con-
stitution of the world. Thou, Lord, hast created the earth,
thou who art ever faithful in all generations, just in thy
judgments, wonderful in thy strength and greatness, wise
in creating, prudent in establishing thy works, kindly in
the things that are seen, faithful towards those who trust
in thee, merciful and compassionate. Forgive us our sins
and our failing, our faults and our shortcomings.

Remember not all the sins of thy servants and hand-
maids, but cleanse us with the cleansing of thy truth and
guide our steps in holiness of heart, that we may do what
is right and pleasing in thine eyes, and in the eyes of our
princes. Yes, sovereign Master, let thy face shine upon
us, that we may enjoy our goods in peace and be protected by thy mighty hand, delivered from every sin by
thy uplifted arm, saved from those who hate us unjustly.

Give concord and peace to us and to all the dwellers
upon earth, as thou didst grant it to our fathers, when
they prayed to thee in faith and truth, obedient to thy
supreme power and holiness.

It is thou, sovereign Master, who hast given power and
kingship to our princes and rulers on the earth, through
thy wonderful and ineffable power, so that we, acknowl-
edging the glory and honour thou hast entrusted to them,
may be subject to them, never opposing thy will. Grant
them, O Lord, health, peace, concord and stability, so
that they may wield without error the sovereignty thou
hast granted them; for it is thou, heavenly Master and
King of the ages, who conferrest on the sons of men
glory, honour and power over the things upon earth.
Lord, guide their counsels according to what is good and
pleasing in thine eyes, so that in piety, peace and gentleness they may administer the authority thou hast given
them, and so obtain thy favour.

Thou alone hast power to accomplish these things and

to give us yet greater blessings. To thee we render thanks through the high Priest and Protector of our souls, Jesus Christ, through whom be given to thee glory and majesty, now, and from generation to generation, for ever and ever! Amen. (St Clement of Rome, *Letter to the Corinthians,* 59-61.)

Ignatius of Antioch († about 107):
The Hymn of God the Father

Your presbytery is tuned to its bishop, like the strings to a lyre, and thus in your concord and harmonious love Christ Jesus is praised. And you too, the rank and file, have become a choir which, singing all in unison, takes up the song from God, and all together you sound it forth, with one voice, through Jesus Christ to the praise of the Father, and so he will both hear you and recognize you in your good works as the members of his Son. (*To the Ephesians,* 4.)

Christian Prayer

Conform all your ways to those of God; reverence one another, and let no one regard his neighbour with the eyes of nature, but love one another always in Christ Jesus. Allow nothing among you which might divide you, but let your union with your bishop and those who preside over you be a pattern and a lesson of eternal life.

Never believe that you can do anything good separately; nothing is good but what you do in common. One prayer in common, one supplication, one spirit, one single hope in charity and innocent joy; for this is Jesus Christ, there is nothing better.

Hasten to meet all together in the one Temple of God, around the one Altar which is Jesus Christ alone, who alone came forth from the Father, always united to him yet returning to him. (*To the Magnesians,* 6, 7.)

His own prayer

I am God's wheat; may I be ground by the teeth of wild beasts that I may become the pure bread of Christ.

My passions have been crucified, and there is not in me any sensuous fire, but a spring rising up in me and murmuring within me: Come to the Father. (*To the Romans,* 4, 7.)

Invocations

Only now do I begin to be a disciple.

May no created thing, seen or unseen, try to cheat me of possessing Jesus Christ. Come fire and cross, wild beasts, hacking, cutting, wrenching of bones, crushing of my whole body, let the cruellest tortures invented by the devil fall upon me; only let me attain to Jesus Christ.

Worthless to me are the charms of the world and the kingdoms of this age. It is better that I die, so as to possess Jesus Christ, than to reign over the ends of the earth. Him I seek, who died for us; him I desire, who rose again for us. Now I feel the birthpangs. Bear with me, brethren, do not hinder me from coming to life, do not seek my death; do not hand over to the world and material temptations one who seeks only to be God's; allow me to receive the pure light; when I arrive there I shall be a man. Let me imitate the passion of my God. If any man has God within him, let him understand what it is I aspire to; let him sympathize with me, since he knows what anguish is laid on me. (*To the Romans,* 5, 6.)

THE SECOND CENTURY MARTYRDOMS

This is the first great wave of martyrs. The story of the Lyons martyrs (177) is well known: here are some others.

Polycarp: at Smyrna, A.D. 156

The Church of God which resides at Smyrna to the Church of God residing at Philomelium and to all Churches which in any place form part of the Holy and Catholic Church: may the mercy, peace and love of God the Father and of our Lord Jesus Christ be with you abundantly.

We are writing to you, brethren, about those who have borne their witness and especially the blessed Polycarp, who by his martyrdom has, as it were, set his seal to the persecution and put an end to it. All the events which preceded his martyrdom happened only to let the Lord of heaven show us a pattern of martyrdom according to the gospel. Polycarp waited to be betrayed, like our Lord, in order to teach us too to imitate him, by not regarding our own private interests but rather that of others. For true and effective charity means that everyone should look not only to his own salvation but to that of all his brethren.

Blessed and heroic were all the examples reported; they were so according to the will of God, for they make us ascribe our advance in holiness to God, whose power is supreme and universal. Who could fail to admire the courage of these confessors, their endurance and love to God? They were so torn with scourges that the anatomy of their bodies was exposed to the very veins and arteries. Yet they stood fast, so that the spectators pitied them and wept for them. Some, again, had reached such heroism of soul that neither cry nor groan escaped them. Seeing them, we realized that while they were being tortured they were no longer in the flesh, or rather that the Lord himself was strengthening them by his presence.

Their minds fixed on the grace of Christ, they despised the torments of the world: in an hour they gained eternal

life. To them the very fire was cold, the fire of those
inhuman torturers; they had before their eyes another
fire, one to be escaped, the everlasting fire which shall
never be quenched. With their mind's eye they gazed on
those good things reserved for those who have suffered,
which the ear has not heard, the eye has not seen, the
heart of man has not conceived. The Lord showed these
things to them, as being already not men but angels.
Finally, condemned to the beasts, the confessors were
made to suffer appalling torments. They were stretched
on sharp shells, they were subjected to all kinds of tortures, so that by the length of their sufferings they might
be induced to deny their faith.

Many were the devices contrived against them by the
devil but, thanks be to God, he could not overcome one
of them. Germanicus, bravest of them all, strengthened
the timidity of the others with the example of his courage.
In the fight with the beasts he was magnificent. The proconsul begged him to have pity on his own youth; Germanicus drew his fierce beast on to himself by striking
it, the sooner to flee from these unjust and criminal
people. The whole crowd, astonished at the bravery and
loyalty of the Christian people, began to shout: "Death
to the atheists! Search out Polycarp!"

There was only one who weakened, Quintus, a Phrygian, lately come from his country. At the sight of the
beasts he was frightened. Now it was he who had wanted
to denounce himself and urged the others to denounce
themselves voluntarily with him. The proconsul succeeded
by his persistence in making him abjure and sacrifice.
Therefore, brethren, we do not approve those who volun-
teer to give themselves up, since that is not the teaching
of the gospel.

The most praiseworthy of the martyrs was Polycarp.
At first, hearing all that had happened, he was not

alarmed, and even wanted to remain in the city. But urged by the majority he at last set out and retired to a small farm, not far from the city, where he stayed with some friends. Night and day, as was his custom, he prayed for all men and for the Churches of the whole world. During his prayer he had a vision: he saw his pillow in flames. Then he came to his friends and said: "I shall be burned alive."

As the chase grew hotter he changed his hiding-place. No sooner had he left than the police arrived; finding him gone they seized two young slaves, one of whom, when put to the torture, gave information. Betrayed by his own servants, he could no longer remain hidden. The irenarch (the chief of police), who was providentially called Herod, was in a hurry to bring him to the arena, where Polycarp was to fulfil his destiny by sharing the fate of Christ, while those who had betrayed him shared the fate of Judas.

So then, on Friday, taking with them the young slave, about supper-time, the police set out, mounted and on foot, armed to the teeth, as if they were out to catch a brigand. Late in the evening they all arrived at the house where Polycarp was. He was lying down in a room on the upper floor; from there he could still have reached another place, but he would not: he simply said: "God's will be done." Hearing the voices of the police, he came down and began to talk with them. They were filled with wonder at his great age and his calmness; they could not understand why they should have taken all this trouble to arrest so old a man. Late as it was, Polycarp made haste to serve them with food and drink, as much as they desired. He only asked them to give him an hour in which to pray undisturbed. They agreed and he proceeded to pray, standing up, as a man filled with the grace of God. And so for two hours, unable to stop, he continued to pray aloud. His hearers were amazed; many were sorry that they had come out against such a godly old man.

When he had finished his prayer, in which he made mention of all he had known in his long life, great and small, known and unknown, and for the Catholic Church throughout the world, the hour for his departure had come. He was mounted on an ass and led towards the city of Smyrna. It was the day of the great sabbath.

On the way he met Herod the chief of police, and his father Nicetas, who seated him in their carriage. There, sitting beside him, they tried to persuade him, saying: "What harm is there in saying 'Lord Caesar,' in sacrificing and so on, in order to save your life?" At first Polycarp would not answer, but when they insisted he declared: "I will not do as you advise." Disappointed, the two men insulted him and pushed him out of their carriage so roughly that he bruised his leg. He took no notice of it, just as if he had felt nothing; cheerfully and briskly he resumed his way on foot. The group moved towards the arena, where the uproar was so loud that no one could make himself heard.

Just as Polycarp entered the stadium a voice from heaven was heard: "Courage, Polycarp, play the man!" No one knew who had spoken, but those of our people who were present heard the voice. As they brought Polycarp forward, great was the tumult on learning that the bishop was arrested. When he stood before the proconsul, the latter asked if he were Polycarp, and hearing that he was, tried to persuade him to deny his faith. "Have respect for your age," he said, and other such things, as the magistrates always say. He added: "Swear by the fortune of Caesar, change your mind, say: Down with the atheists!"

Polycarp looked gravely on the crowd of godless heathens who filled the arena, pointed to them with his hand and groaned, then raised his eyes to heaven and said: "Down with the atheists!"

Again the proconsul pressed him, saying: "Take the oath and I will release you. Insult Christ."

"Six and eighty years now have I served him," replied Polycarp, "and he has never done me wrong. How then should I blaspheme my King and Saviour?"

The proconsul insisted, repeating: "Swear by the fortune of Caesar." "You flatter yourself," the bishop answered, "if you hope to make me swear by the fortune of Caesar, as you say: if you pretend not to know what I am, hear my frank avowal: I am a Christian. If you want to know what the teaching of Christianity is, appoint me a day and hear me."

The proconsul said: "Speak to the people," but Polycarp answered: "Before you I should think it right to explain myself, for we are taught to give to magistrates and the authorities appointed by God the honour due to them, so far as these marks of respect do not offend against our faith."

"I have wild beasts," said the proconsul, "unless you retract I will deliver you to them." "Give your orders," the bishop said, "As for us, when we change, it is not from better to worse; but it is noble to change from evil to good."

The proconsul said: "Since you scorn the beasts, I will put you to death by fire, if you do not change your mind." But Polycarp replied: "You threaten me with a fire which burns for a time and then goes out. But do you know the fire of the judgement to come? Do you know the chastisement which will devour the wicked? Come, waste no more time! Decide as you will!"

Polycarp gave these and other answers with joy and courage, his face shining with divine grace. It was not he who was disturbed by the interrogation but the proconsul, who now sent his herald to make this proclamation thrice in the middle of the arena: "Polycarp has confessed to being a Christian."

At these words the crowd of Jews and pagans living in Smyrna could not contain their fury and roared: "There he is, the teacher of Asia, the father of the Christians, the destroyer of our gods! It is his teaching that stops so many from paying them sacrifice and worship."

In the midst of this uproar Philip the Asiarch (minister of public worship) was asked to set a lion on Polycarp, but he forbade it: the hunting sports were now closed. "To the fire, then!" they shouted from every side. The vision of a few days before was now to be fulfilled, when in his prayer the old man had seen his pillow burned in the flames, and had told the faithful with him: "I shall be burned alive."

All this happened in less time than it takes to tell. The mob ran to heap up logs and firewood taken from the workshops and bath-furnaces, the Jews in particular distinguishing themselves, as usual, by their zeal. When the pyre was ready, Polycarp took off his clothes, undid his girdle and prepared also to take off his shoes. This was something he did not usually have to do, for the faithful who were about him would hasten to help him and see who could be the first to touch him; so honoured was he for his great holiness, even before his martyrdom.

At once, then, they arranged round him the things needed to fasten him to the stake. The executioners were for nailing him, but he said: "Let me be. He who has given me strength to face the fire will give me strength also to stand still at the stake, without need of your nails." So they did not nail him but only tied him. Bound to the stake, his hands behind his back, Polycarp seemed like a choice ram, towering above a large flock, ready for sacrifice. Then, raising his eyes, he said:

"Lord God almighty, Father of Jesus Christ, thy beloved and blessed Son, through whom we have known thee; God of angels and powers, God of all creation and of the whole family of the just who live in thy presence; I bless thee for counting me worthy of this day and this hour, worthy to be numbered among thy martyrs and to share in the cup of thy Christ, to rise again to the eternal life of body and soul in the immortality of the Holy Spirit.

May I be accepted today with them in thy presence as a precious and pleasing victim, as thou hast warned me and shown me; for thou hast kept thy promise, O God of faithfulness and truth. For this grace and for all things I praise thee, I bless thee, I glorify thee through the eternal high priest in the heavens, Jesus Christ, thy beloved Son, through whom be glory given to thee, together with him and the Holy Spirit, now and to all ages, Amen."

When Polycarp had uttered this *Amen* at the end of his prayer, the men in charge of the fire lit it and the flames rose high and flaring. Then we witnessed a wonder, and we were spared so that we might tell the tale to others. The fire rose in the form of a vault, or like a sail bellying in the wind, and surrounded the martyr's body. The bishop stood in the middle, not as burning flesh, but like a loaf being baked brown, or as gold and silver in the crucible. All this time we could smell a delicious aroma, like incense or precious spices.

At last these wicked men, seeing that the fire could not destroy the body, sent an executioner to smite him with the sword. There came out [a dove, and] blood which flowed so abundantly that the fire was at once put out. The whole crowd was astonished at the difference between the infidels and the elect. Among these we reckon the incomparable martyr Polycarp who was our master among us, filled with the spirit of the apostles and prophets, bishop of the Catholic Church of Smyrna. All the words of his mouth have been or will be fulfilled.

But the devil, our envious and wicked adversary, enemy of the race of the just, had seen the splendour of Polycarp's martyrdom: he knew of his blameless life since childhood, and now saw him crowned with immortality as the reward of an unchallenged victory. He schemed to prevent us taking away even the martyr's body, as many would have wished to do, so as to share his precious relics. So the devil suggested to Nicetas, Herod's father and Alce's brother, to plead with the consul, that he should not give us the body. "There is a risk," he said, "that the Christians may abandon the Crucified to worship Polycarp."

He said this at the instigation of the Jews who were mounting guard over the pyre and saw that we intended to draw the body out of the fire. They did not know that we could never abandon Christ, who suffered for all souls saved throughout the world, the innocent for the guilty; never could we worship another. We worship Christ as the Son of God; the martyrs we honour as disciples and imitators of Christ. We love them as they deserve to be loved, because of their unsurpassable love for their King and Master. May we be made their companions and disciples!

Seeing the bitterness of the Jews, the centurion put the body in the middle of the fire and caused it to be burnt up, according to the custom of the heathen. It was only later that we were able to carry away Polycarp's bones, more precious than jewels, purer than refined gold. We laid them in a fitting place. There we shall assemble whenever possible in joy and gladness, and the Lord will allow us to celebrate the anniversary of his servant's martyrdom, to commemorate those who have already fought their fight, to train and prepare their successors.

Such is the story of the blessed Polycarp. He suffered martyrdom at Smyrna, with eleven companions, natives of Philadelphia, but he is the one who has a special place in our memory. All men, even the pagans, are talking about him everywhere. Not only was he an eminent teacher but also a martyr without compare, whose martyrdom all desire to imitate, because it was a faithful copy of that of Christ, recorded in the Gospel. By his endurance he overcame the wicked judge and obtained the crown of immortality. Now with the apostles and the saints, in joy he glorifies God the Father almighty, he blesses our Lord Jesus Christ, the Saviour of our souls, the Captain of our bodies, the Shepherd of the Catholic Church spread abroad through the whole world.

You asked us to give you a detailed account of all that took place. We are sending you this summary report by the hand of our brother Marcion. When you have read it, kindly pass on the letter to the brethren farther away, so that they in turn may give glory to God for having raised up his elect among his servants.

To God, who by a gift of his grace is able to lead us all to his heavenly kingdom, through his only-begotten Son Jesus Christ, be glory, honour, power and majesty for ever and ever! Greet all the saints. Those who are with us greet you; so does Evaristus the scribe, with all his family.

Polycarp suffered martyrdom on the second day of the month Xanthicus, seven days before the Kalends of March, on the day of the great sabbath, at the eighth hour. He was arrested by Herod, when Philip of Tralles was high priest and Statius Quadratus was proconsul of the province of Asia, during the unending reign of our Lord Jesus Christ: to him be given glory, honour, majesty and eternal kingship, from generation to generation! Amen.

We beseech you, brethren, to walk according to the word of our Lord Jesus Christ, preserved in the gospel. Glory be to him with the Father and the Holy Spirit, because he has saved the saints called by him, as he has given martyrdom to his blessed Polycarp. Following him, may we come to the kingdom of our Lord Jesus Christ!

All this has been written from the copy belonging to Irenaeus, by Gaius, who lived a long time with Irenaeus, a disciple of Polycarp.

I, Socrates of Corinth, have transcribed this from the copy of Gaius. Grace be with you all!

And I, Pionius, have written all this, from the aforesaid copy. I had searched for it, but the blessed Polycarp revealed it to me, as I shall relate elsewhere. I have collected these facts, which time had almost caused to be forgotten, in order that our Lord Jesus Christ may join me also to his elect in the heavenly kingdom. To him, with the Father and the Holy Spirit, be glory for ever and ever! Amen.

Justin: at Rome, A.D. 163

(Martyrdom of the holy martyrs Justin, Chariton, Charito, Euelpistus, Hierax, Paeon and Liberian.)

In the time when the wicked defenders of idolatry were in full fury, impious decrees against the pious Christians were published in town and country alike, in order to force them to offer libations in honour of vain idols.

So the saints were arrested together and brought before the prefect of Rome, by name Rusticus. When they stood before the tribunal, Rusticus the prefect said to Justin: "First, submit to the gods and obey the emperors."

Justin: No one can be blamed or condemned for obeying the commands of our Saviour, Jesus Christ.

Rusticus: What philosophy do you profess?

Justin: I have studied all philosophies in turn, but at last I have adhered to the true doctrine of the Christians, whether it pleases those who have been led astray by false doctrine or no.

Rusticus: And does this philosophy please you, wretched man?

Justin: Yes, because I adhere to the true doctrine, following the Christians.

Rusticus: What is this doctrine?

Justin: We adore the God of the Christians: we believe that this God is the only God, that from the beginning he is the Creator and Artificer of the whole universe, of things visible and invisible. We believe that Jesus Christ, the Son of God, is Lord: foretold by the prophets as coming to help the race of men, herald of salvation and teacher of right knowledge. I, being but a man, am too frail, I confess, to speak worthily of his infinite Godhead: I realize that for this a prophetic power is needed. But the prophecies exist, concerning him of whom I have just spoken as the Son of God, for the prophets were inspired from on high when they told his coming among men.

Rusticus: Where do you meet?

Justin: Wherever each one wills and is able. Do you suppose, then, that we all meet in the same place? Not at all: the God of the Christians is not confined to one place. He is invisible: he fills heaven and earth; everywhere he is worshipped and glorified by the faithful.

Rusticus: Answer me now: where do you meet? Where do you gather your disciples?

Justin: I live over one Martin, near the bath of Timothy. During all this time—and this is the second time I have come to live in Rome—I know of no other meeting-place. To all who have come to find me there I have taught the doctrine of the truth.

Rusticus: You are a Christian, then?

Justin: Yes, I am a Christian.

Rusticus now said to Chariton: "Now, Chariton, are you a Christian?"

Chariton: I am a Christian, by the will of God.

Rusticus (to Charito, a woman): And you, Charito, what do you answer?

Charito: So am I, by the grace of God.

Rusticus (to Euelpistus) And what are you?

Euelpistus (a slave of Caesar): I am a Christian too. I was emancipated by Christ: I share the same hope, by the grace of Christ.

Rusticus (to Hierax): You too, are you a Christian?

Hierax: Yes, I am a Christian. I worship and adore the same God.

Rusticus: Did Justin make you a Christian?

Hierax: I have always been a Christian, and always will be.

A man called Paeon stood up and said: "I too am a Christian."

Rusticus: Who taught you?

Paeon: I received this holy doctrine from my parents.

Euelpistus: Of course I listened gladly to Justin's lessons, but I too owe it to my parents that I am a Christian.

Rusticus: Where are your parents?

Euelpistus: In Cappadocia.

Rusticus: And where are yours, Hierax?

Hierax: Our true father is Christ; our mother is the faith, by which we believe in him. Our earthly parents are dead. I belong to Iconium in Phrygia; I was carried off from there and came here.

Rusticus (to Liberian): And what have you to say for yourself? Are you too one of the unbelievers?

Liberian: I too am a Christian. I am not an unbeliever, but I worship the one true God.

Rusticus (to Justin): Listen, you who are supposed to be learned, and think you have the true doctrine: if I have you scourged and then beheaded, are you sure that you will then ascend to heaven?

Justin: I trust that I shall have my dwelling there, if I endure all this, and I know that the divine reward is reserved, till the end of the whole world, for all who have lived thus.

Rusticus: Do you fancy, then, that you will ascend to heaven to receive certain rewards?

Justin: I do not fancy it, I am convinced of it, I am certain.

Rusticus: Get back to facts. Come to the point we demand of you, which is urgent. Approach together, all of you, and sacrifice to the gods.

Justin: No man in his senses will leave piety for impiety.

Rusticus: If you do not obey, you will be tortured without mercy.

Justin: That is our dearest wish, to suffer for our Lord Jesus Christ, so that we may be saved. That will be our salvation and confidence before the dreadful judgement-seat of our Lord and Saviour, before whom the whole world will stand to be judged.

The other martyrs all said the same: "Do what you will. We are Christians and we do not sacrifice to idols."

Rusticus the prefect then pronounced sentence: "Let those who have refused to sacrifice to the gods and obey the orders of the emperor be scourged and led away to be beheaded, according to the laws."

The holy martyrs praised God and were then led out to the usual place of execution. There they were beheaded, thus consummating martyrdom in the confession of our Saviour.

Some of the faithful carried off their bodies by stealth and laid them in a fitting place, sustained by the grace of our Lord Jesus Christ, to whom be glory for ever and ever! Amen.

CHAPTER III

DOCTRINAL DEVELOPMENTS AND THE ORGANIZATION OF THE CHURCH IN THE SECOND CENTURY

During the first century after the Church of Christ had been established in Rome and begun to suffer attacks of different kinds, this still youthful Christianity had proved itself active, strong and vigorous. It had held fast against the intermittent but cruel outbreaks of persecution and the peril constantly menacing the faithful ever since Nero. But meanwhile its own proper life, both in the inner order of the spirit and in the organization necessary to maintain it, never ceased to grow stronger.

The first victory of its spirit was won against a formidable peril which threatened its very essence: the speculative system known as Gnosticism which tended to substitute for the simple, living teaching of Christ a mass of sterile, baseless doctrines which would have totally altered its nature. With these went a condemnation of the work of creation and a contempt for the flesh which might produce either unbridled license (since nothing carnal is of any account) or, on the contrary, a rigid asceticism, forbidding all contacts supposed to be unclean, such as the use of certain foods and even marriage. The trenchant warnings of St Paul and then of the apostolic Fathers, especially St Ignatius of Antioch, exorcized the danger.

St Clement of Rome seems not to have had occasion to condemn Gnosticism directly, but his solid Roman commonsense was utterly opposed to such excesses. His letter to the Corinthians shows him to have been more concerned for charity than for speculations. With his ability to recognize the good qualities of Jews and pagans who had lived exemplary lives, there is a breath of human kindness about him which is bound up with his admiration for the work of God, "sovereign Creator and Lord of the universe, who has willed that all the world should abide in concord and peace." So the Christian should respond to the divine intention by the constant practice of charity, "which unites us intimately to God" and in which "is consummated the perfection of all the elect of God."

St Ignatius, in his letters to the various Churches of Asia Minor, struck back with all his might at the fantasies of the Gnostics, which went the length of denying the reality of the life of Jesus Christ, the very source of the Christian's life. This life is manifested in the Church, which is not just a comity of scattered communities, but a real unity created by Christ and represented in each of them by the bishop. "Where the bishop is, there the people must be, just as where Jesus Christ is, there is the Catholic Church." This unity rests on the eminent dignity of the Roman Church, which Ignatius describes as "president of the charity," that is, of the brotherhood of all Christians, who are all one in Christ. They are intensely conscious of belonging to Christ, who is God, sole mediator and sole source of life, and not to the hierarchies of intermediary spirits imagined by the Gnostics. This is really the essence of Ignatius' teaching, which leads all things and all men to him who alone gives life, and for whom all must live and even, in order to live, be ready to die. The imminence of that martyrdom he was to suffer at Rome (martyrdom was always present to Ignatius' mind) reveals the depth of that life, the ardour of his desire and the certainty of his faith.

All these aspirations and affirmations are found a little later in St Polycarp, bishop of Smyrna, in a letter—one of his few writings which have survived—to a friend of his boyhood, written to dissuade him from the Gnostic errors. But we know from his disciple St Irenaeus that, like St Paul a century earlier, he had written, among others, to the Christians of the Macedonian town of Philippi, to remind them that for Christians there is no hope save in Christ, "who suffered for us that we might have life in him"; and that it is through the apostles and no others that his teaching has been handed on. Polycarp, who was venerated by the whole Church, longed to be its witness in his turn, and his dearest wish was therefore to seal his witness with his blood. All his life he longed for martyrdom, though never seeking it, according to the invariable teaching of the Church, always opposed to self-sought martyrdom. But when, in the reign of Marcus Aurelius, there was an outbreak of antichristian fanaticism, which bore heavily on the Church of Smyrna, and the mob clamoured for his death, the proconsul of Asia condemned him to the stake and he died, blessing the Lord, surrounded by his admiring flock.

After Clement of Rome, disciple of St Peter, after Polycarp of Smyrna, who had known St John, the line of witnesses of the apostolic Fathers was crowned at the end of the second century by Irenaeus, a disciple of Polycarp, who became bishop of Lyons. Succeeding in Gaul to St Pothinus, whom he had accompanied or rejoined, yet always keeping in touch with his native land, he personified, in a western world now awakening to the Christian faith, the thought of the East whence he came. In his Greek writings, such as *Against the Heretics,* as well as in his preaching in the Celtic language which he had learned so as to be understood by his Gaulish flock, he repeated always the same truth as his predecessors, that salvation is in Jesus Christ alone. From the ravings of the Gnostics, as from those of the Montanists (Phrygian visionaries who said they were directly inspired by the Holy Ghost and were disturbing the Churches in both east and west) he appeals to Scripture and to tradition, to which he is a well-qualified witness, since he too, in his youth, had personally known the "Elders" or Presbyters, who had conversed with the Lord's companions. This tradition of the apostles, he says, is manifest in all the Churches, but especially in that Church, known by all from the beginning, "which has been established in Rome by the two glorious apostles, Peter and Paul . . . With this Church, because of its superior pre-eminence, every Church must be in agreement, that is, those who are the faithful everywhere." [1] And so Irenaeus, a firsthand witness to the authentic tradition of the Christian East, which he maintains against the fantasies of the Gnostics, contributes by his teaching to planting its roots firmly in that privileged centre which he has visited and which, from being capital of the empire, has become the providential spot where was consummated the joint apostolate of St Peter and St Paul.

Thus, in the course of the first two centuries that one faith in Christ, and the teachings of those who had been

---

[1] The Latin text reads: *Ad hanc enim ecclesiam, propter potentiorem principlatitatem necesse est omnem convenire ecclesiam, hoc est eos qui sunt undique fideles, in qua semper ab his qui sunt undique conservata est ea quae est ab apostolis traditio.*

commissioned to hand it on, was asserted with unfailing continuity. But it is no passive faith. Whoever professes it becomes a new man, his life is transformed. Alongside the apostolic Fathers, Clement of Rome, Ignatius and Polycarp, who hand on a doctrine always the same yet ever enriched from its own depths, Hermas, brother of Pope Pius I (about 140-54), in his rather incoherent but very vivid book *The Shepherd,* lays stress on these obligations of the Christian life, expounded in a series of visions, commandments and parables. The Christian must beware of effeminacy and lukewarmness, which spring from contact with the world, and of anxiety over worldly business and wealth, the possession of which is not illicit, but full of dangers. The Christian must distrust them and all worldly ambitions, which breed discord. In a community of brethren, composed largely of humble folk, the man who is proud and jealous for his own prosperity will be out of his element, if he wants to be faithful to God.

But Christians are not always faithful. There are some who commit sin, which can only be washed away by penance. In principle, penance is given by baptism, which does away with all past evil. After baptism there ought to be no more question of sin. But in fact this is not so, and the Lord, "knowing the weakness of men and the malice of the devil," has instituted another source of penance, which is dispensed by the Church. It can even be repeated, since lapses are unhappily not exceptional. Yet it is true that if a man is in the habit of doing wrong, "falling again repeatedly into sin, only to do penance again, his salvation seems indeed doubtful."

Such is the grandeur and rigour of the Christian ideal, which regards a grave sin after baptism as an unworthy lapse, not to be tolerated indefinitely. Yet there is pardon for the penitent sinner, even if he sins often and repents often, provided he can plead a sincere and strong resolution. Here, from the lips of one close to the supreme bishop, we learn the exacting yet merciful doctrine taught by the *Shepherd* about the middle of the second century, in which the sense for reality always found at Rome does not violate the purity of its principles.

To avoid falling into sin, rather to draw ever nearer to our Lord, the sovereign means is prayer. In the private life of all Christians, as in the corporate life of the Church, the importance of prayer is capital. Did not St Paul teach his disciples to pray without ceasing? This means that their hearts must constantly be turned to God. But at certain hours, not rigorously fixed, though the morning, midday and evening are naturally indicated, they are to offer to God a more explicit prayer of adoration, praise and petition. What the Christian does in private the Christian community does collectively, at the times it has fixed. It is a prayer which derives originally from Jewish prayer, of which we find echoes in the hymns preserved in the Gospels, the *Magnificat* and the *Benedictus,* and even in the Lord's prayer. But our Lord has renewed prayer by the wholly filial accent he has given it. Can we say that Jesus revolutionized prayer? No, but he has transfigured it by giving us examples of it in his own converse with his Father. The Christian in turn approaches his heavenly Father in the name of his Son Jesus Christ, the one Mediator, as we see in the great prayer which concludes the Letter of St Clement and is addressed to "the Creator of the universe, through his well-beloved Son Jesus Christ." But it is also addressed to Christ himself, as is attested by the most ancient hymns, and noted by a pagan author like Pliny the Younger, who wrote: "The Christians are accustomed to meet at a fixed hour before the dawn and to sing a hymn in honour of Christ as a god, in alternating chants."

This is the official prayer of the Church, ritual and

liturgical, accompanied in practice by hymns of praise, but the heart of it is the celebration of the Eucharistic mystery, the oblation of Jesus Christ, Son of God, to his Father, in the symbolic meal, in which all the faithful partake by communion.

In his *Apology,* a defence of the faith addressed to the emperor, the philosopher Justin, a Christian writer of the time of Marcus Aurelius, gives a most explicit description of this liturgy, which then and for some time to come was not intended to be revealed to those outside:

> On the day which is called the Sun's day there is an assembly of all who live in the towns or the country: and the memoirs of the apostles or the writings of the prophets are read, as much as time permits. When the reader has finished, the president gives a discourse, admonishing us and exhorting us to imitate these excellent examples. Then we all rise together and offer prayers: and, as I said before, on the conclusion of our prayer, bread is brought, and wine and water: and the president similarly offers up prayers and thanksgivings to the best of his power, and the people assent with *Amen.* Then follows the distribution of the eucharistic gifts ["eucharisted things"—things over which thanks have been offered] and the partaking of them by all: and they are sent to the absent by the hands of the deacons. (*Apologia* I, 67, Trans. H. Bettenson)

All the essentials of the Mass are there.

From Justin, too, we have a description of the liturgy of baptism, which brings into the Church of Christ one who does not yet belong to it. It is preceded by obligatory prayer and fasting, then the neophyte is led to a place where there is water, in which he is plunged three times, for "they then make their ablution in the water in the name of the Father, Lord of all, and of our Saviour Jesus Christ and of the Holy Spirit" (*Ibid.* 61).

From apostolic times this confession of the divine Trinity was inseparable from the rite of baptism, and the neophytes were only admitted to it after a profession of faith, which is that bequeathed by Christ to his apostles. It is the nucleus of what came to be called, for this reason, the Apostles' Creed, which is simply the development of it, expressing the whole faith of the Church, the same in all places. "This faith, sworn to by the Christian at baptism, is his most precious treasure and at the same time his password, or *tessera,* which will lead to his being recognized everywhere as a son of the Catholic [that is, universal] Church, and as one of Christ's faithful. He may, like St Irenaeus, be born and grow up at Smyrna, live in Rome and evangelize the Gauls; but he will find everywhere the same faith and will be everywhere illumined by the same sun of God." [2]

It is this profound unity of belief which makes the unity of the Church. But this unity is shown also in her organization. In the very earliest days this organization was confined to its essentials but it was gradually strengthened and diversified, never ceasing to be essentially alive. The Church, a society of those who, sharing the same faith in Christ, love him and are loved by him and, for love of him, love one another, constitutes above all a brotherhood, an *agape* or charity, in St Ignatius' phrase, of which unity is the fruit. Therefore, in the world in which they are gradually spreading, Christians form but one body, just as they form a single whole in each place. But unity is inseparable from a hierarchy, and so from the beginning we see each unit represented by the council of the Presbyters or Elders, itself subordinate to the founder apostle, or to those who represent him or carry on his work, and whose title of "bishop," from the Greek *episkopos* or

[2] J. Lebreton, *History of the Primitive Church,* Vol. II, p. 297. See Select Bibliography at the end of this volume.

supervisor, signifies that this community is entrusted to their overseeing. The collegiate organization of ecclesiastical government, typical of most of the Churches known in the primitive period, does not exclude the unity of the ruling authority. The presbyteral college, composed of priests or elders, forms the bishop's council and assists him in his litugical and teaching functions, taking his place when necessary.

In the earliest days the second order of bishop's assistants, the deacons or servers, played a more distinct and autonomous but more limited part. The deacons were the active liturgical auxiliaries of the Christian community. They distributed Holy Communion and gave baptism with the bishop's permission, but above all they helped him in administration, especially in the management of the community's property, a considerable part of which was devoted to the needs of the poor, the deacon being always the minister of charity. Further, during the age when Christianity had only reached the urban centres of the Roman world and so was concentrated mainly in the towns, the bishop of each town concentrated in himself practically all sacerdotal functions, so that the diaconal body was more apparently obvious than the presbyteral, and it often happened that the senior deacon succeeded the bishop on his death.

In the primitive Church there were also certain female collaborators of the deacons: the deaconesses, both virgins and widows, mentioned in some of St Paul's epistles, who devoted themselves to the care of the sick and needy and the education of the children, but this institution soon disappeared.

On the other hand, some teachers appointed for religious instruction, *didaskaloi* or doctors, often had a prominent rôle. They were in reality catechists, who in some Churches had only private authority, but in others were under the direct control of ecclesiastical authority and had the character of an official institution.

In the first Christian age there were also "prophets," of whom St Paul speaks favourably. But these free preachers of doctrine, whose personal spiritual gifts might appear opposed to the commands of the hierarchy, were not long in provoking a rather natural distrust, and they soon ceased to play a recognized part.

It was, then, the bishop, the presbyteral college and the deacons who alone constituted the clergy in the proper sense, and were very soon distinguished from the rest of the faithful by the fact that they exercized functions not open to all, as these required certain special qualifications. Those, for instance, whom St Paul's Epistles to Timothy and Titus call "bigamists," that is, who had married more than once, were excluded from the clergy. In the first two centuries, however, there was no question of the obligation of celibacy. St Paul's preferences for that state were certainly obvious and could claim in support the example of Christ himself, but the high regard in which continence was held did not go to the length of imposing it on aspirants for Holy Orders. But at an early date those who had received ordination to the priesthood when still unmarried were barred from marriage. From the second century the state of virginity was highly honoured in the Church, and the idea soon took root of preferring for ordination those who had preserved it.

The choice of the first clerics had belonged to the apostles, that of their successors to those who succeeded the apostles. But the opinion of the ordinary faithful was not without influence on this choice and, after the deaths of the first heads, it was the communities themselves who nominated their new pastors. The bishops were thus chosen by their Churches, but they were usually proposed by the clergy of the episcopal city, the choice being confirmed by the people. The episcopal character itself could only be transmitted through the consecration of the newly-elect by a bishop already in office.

At the end of the second century the number of bishops still varied greatly in different regions. They were numerous in Syria, Palestine and Asia Minor, but Egypt for a long time had only one, who came to be called the Patriarch of Alexandria; in Italy it appears that outside Rome there were only the sees of Milan and Ravenna. Nearly the whole of Gaul was still grouped under the jurisdiction of the bishop of Lyons, while about the organization of the infant Church of Spain we possess very little information.

But Rome, seat of the empire, where St Peter, preceded by St Paul, had established himself, the place subsequently adorned by a man like St Clement, enjoyed an unrivalled prestige. Writing to the successors of Peter and Paul, St Ignatius of Antioch said: "You have never deceived anyone; you have taught others: I desire that all you enjoin in your teaching may remain uncontested." The well-known epitaph of Abercius, a Phrygian bishop contemporary with Marcus Aurelius, salutes in poetic vein the "royal majesty of the Roman Church, the queen in vestments of gold," and from all parts of the Christian world it is to Rome that men turn when they seek authentic witnesses to apostolic tradition. The names of the bishops of the Roman Church, carefully preserved in lists going back uninterruptedly to St Peter, made it possible to confront innovators with the antiquity of tradition as taught by the apostles.

Everywhere, then, the same faith was maintained, the same life was nourished by it. The Christian life, whatever its special features in different surroundings, regions or social groups, is one in its source, and everywhere the Christian is revealed by the same traits.

But the Christian does not try to isolate himself. The author of a precious document of the late second century, which is known as the *Epistle to Diognetus,* remarks that believers in Christ do not distinguish themselves from other men by their clothes, food or houses. The Christian writer Tertullian, who in his unorthodox old age did indeed develop more "isolationist" tendencies, says: "We do not live apart from this world; like you we frequent the forum, the baths, the workshops, the shops, the markets and public places; we follow the callings of sailor, soldier, farmer or merchant, we put our work and our skill at your service." "Conscientious objection" to military service is only exceptionally discussed in literature, and was never a common fact in Christian practice. Nonetheless, the close connection in the ancient State between civic life and religious acts was unthinkable for those who wor- shipped one God, or customs condemned by the morality of the Gospel, such as combats in the arena, forced Chris- tians to withdraw from a certain area of social life. This partial moral secession may have been aggravated by the apocalyptic tendencies of certain Christians, inclined to prophesy, if not to prepare for, the ruin of the old order. But the Church's legitimate authorities took no responsibility for such extremism. Only it is true that, to Christians, interests of a merely earthly nature are not of the first importance, and that in varying degrees they professed a relative lack of interest in the social scene and this, somewhat exaggerated, was made a charge against them.

On the other hand, the Christians compensated for this failing on the civic side by the good example of their conduct, one better equipped than that of others to endow human life with its full dignity, that of a life according to the spirit. They abstained from amusements which seemed natural to pagan society, on the ground of their cruelty or indecency. They showed themselves equally indifferent to the advantages of wealth, or at least refused to enjoy them selfishly. They renounced, or at least curtailed, unnecessary expenses and luxury in attire, though there were some who indulged themselves on this head, and the rigorist Tertullian scolds those women who, he thinks, are too taken up with the care of their persons and the choice of clothes. Moderation in the personal use of this world's goods, moderation in moral conduct; these are two distinctive marks of the Christian. Alone among the religions, Christianity holds inexorably to the law proclaimed at Jerusalem in the council of the apostles and always denounces carnal relations outside marriage as gravely sinful in themselves. There was even in some quarters a tendency to reprove second marriages. St Paul, however, had tolerated them and even advised them for young widows. Nonetheless, they were rather frowned upon, since the Church even made them an impediment to the reception of holy Orders.

Christian asceticism is expressed also in fasting, by which the Christian associates himself with the voluntary mortification of Christ in the desert. The faithful of the first two centuries fasted twice a week, on Wednesday, perhaps in reparation for the treachery of Judas, and on Friday in memory of the Passion. Towards the end of the second century the paschal fast began to be added. It included the days immediately before the feast, and was later extended to forty days. During this period, no food was eaten till the ninth hour—about three in the afternoon.

Mortified in his private life, in order to imitate Christ and hold his passions in check, the Christian worthy of the name always seeks only the good of his neighbour. Every member of the Christian community is always at the service of all, and the fulfilment of this duty of charity ranges from almsgiving, which helps his beneficiary not to die of hunger, to encouragement to martyrdom, which helps him to die for Christ. A glorious example of this was given by the martyrs of Lyons, among many others. We know that such a mutual love impressed the pagans, whose saying: "See how these Christians love one another" perhaps reveals a secret envy. Of all the traits of the Christian life, and in spite of the prejudices which slandered it, this is perhaps the one which was most noticed and could only be admired. The chief argument put forward in favour of Christianity by the writers known as apologists, who in the second century began to plead the Christian cause, is precisely the exemplary conduct of its followers.

Pure lives, deep piety, unfaltering loyalty and boundless charity; these things did more, perhaps, for the extension of the kingdom of Christ than the finest discourses aimed at the pagans' conversion.

To such a point did this unique charity refashion the relations of man with man that it ended in fact by rejecting slavery, "making no respect of persons," since the Christian put free men and slaves on the same footing. Even if, on the social and political level, the Church did not begin by condemning an institution which it found established and which seemed natural to nearly everyone, its doctrine of the divine sonship as formulated by St Paul implicitly denied its foundations. On the one hand, for the Christian master the slave was still a man, with the right to the same personal respect as a free man, and on the other hand, and in consequence, slaves in the Christian community were emancipated with increasing frequency. The all-powerful action of the Gospel, proclaiming the universal brotherhood of men in Christ, created a new society without overthrowing institutions all at once.

This universalism forms another of the characteristics of the Christian ideal. It was to become that of the whole world, it embraced all mankind, and the framework of the Roman empire, vast as it was, was itself outstripped. The Church is made for the whole world, whence comes that name of Catholic which is already found in Ignatius, about the year 100.

The greatness of this ideal could not but strike those who did not share it. But while it sometimes compelled admiration, principles of life in some ways so new and in such marked contrast with the easy morality of the age and contrary to accepted social customs, were bound to provoke pagan society to unfavourable reactions, easily turning to violent hostility, inspired with a resolute will to destroy.

The civil authorities might condemn the Christians as men who did not worship the gods of the empire. The cultivated upper classes might look down on them as groups in which the common people were dominant and culture and refinement were of little consideration. But the masses of the people, despite their sometimes admiring wonder at the sight of superhuman charity or unprecedented heroism, instinctively suspected followers of a life apart and dissenters from the common religion, inputing to them faults, vices and secret crimes. It was but a step from suspicion to belief, which was followed closely by accusation.

Atheism, because they did not pay the homage due from all to the gods of Rome; magic, because they celebrated secret ceremonies; perhaps also cannibalism and, by extension, infanticide, from a false idea of the communion of the Body of Christ; scandalous indecencies, a charge always eagerly brought against those whose lives are disapproved of; such were the common libels against them. Combined with these was a less malicious mockery, aimed at the religious practices attributed to the Christians, through some curious confusions, like the supposed worship of a god with an ass's head, making the Christians like the devotees of the Egyptian god Seth, whom a Gnostic sect had compared with Jesus. There is a famous caricature which can be seen on the Palatine Hill in Rome, representing a crucified man with an ass's head, over the caption "Alexamenos adores his god," to which the Christian thus mocked has retorted with the calm affirmation of his faith: "Alexamenos is faithful."

Educated men of the second century held less inexact ideas of Christianity. We still know only too well how easily men and women of the world will accept the most fantastic tales about those who profess ideas not squaring with their own. The dominant attitude in the upper classes of Roman society towards the Christians at that time was, in fact, contempt, tempered sometimes with a little pity or sharpened by irritation, like that of Marcus Aurelius, at their willingness for martyrdom. The cultured were not generally well disposed. The polemics of the philosopher Celsus no doubt give a fair impression of the complex reactions of imperial society towards Christianity, then and for long after. Celsus makes it his chief objection that it is a "barbarous" doctrine, absurd, fitted for uneducated people, from whom it draws most of its members. He charges them equally with "separating themselves from other men and despising the society in which they live." Far from admitting that a higher standard of morality would in the long run benefit the State, he sees the Christian "chimera" only as a public danger, because on points held to be vital it does not square with traditional social structure and civilization. The many pagans who, like him, held the State, as guardian of the national traditions, to be the supreme consideration, could not reconcile themselves to the affirmation that the invisible world is superior to the visible, a doctrine which in their eyes was mischievous and even seditious.

No wonder, then, that being supported by a public opinion inspired by mistrust, contempt and open hostility, the cruel legislation which denied Christians the right to exist, and held over them the constant threat of death, was so long maintained.

This explains why the Christians were constantly thinking of a possible martyrdom and why we find that serene, even joyful acceptance of it, which was one of the marks of Christian life in those early centuries, and was certainly disconcerting to those outside the fold, as it still is to many, even today. The persecutions were actually intermittent only, but at times they were very widespread, and in some areas very frequent. This means that the number of martyrs, though impossible to estimate, was certainly not small. The names of many have certainly not come down to us, and the ancient inscriptions themselves allude to those anonymous heroes whose names, they say, are known only to God, *quorum nomina Deus scit.*

Faced with this perpetual menace, conscious too that they were anything but bad citizens, the Christians naturally conceived the idea of putting forward their case openly, and a certain number took this in hand. Thus, after those earlier authors who had written to instruct their brethren, there appeared others who used their talents to defend them, and are therefore called the Apologists. The author of the *Letter to Diognetus,* a great work which has been described as the pearl of ancient Christian literature, shows how his brethren took part in the common life, not separating from the human, civic community, but only withdrawing from it because of stricter moral standards. After him an Athenian, Marcianus Aristides, a contemporary of the emperor Antoninus, composed an appeal developing the same theme, while at Rome a professional philosopher, St Justin, who taught publicly and died a martyr under Marcus Aurelius, vigorously rebutted the charges of theism, cannibalism and immorality. One of his disciples, Tatian, a native of Assyria, took up the cudgels against pagan errors, and another Athenian, Athenagoras, again vindicated the Christians against current calumnies, in a work full of dignity and serenity, allied with wit. Finally an Asiatic, Theophilus, bishop of Antioch, went over likewise from defence to attack, with a vigour which bordered on narrowmindedness. In this he was very different from the author of the first apologetic in Latin, Minucius Felix, whose little treatise, in the form of a dialogue between two friends, a Christian and a pagan, is full of a charm and kindness which are very attractive. He concludes with a picture of the moral beauty of Christianity, in which all the truth and goodness expressed in Roman thought is found preserved, and indeed surpassed.

But it was not only with external adversaries that the defenders of genuine Christianity had to contend. No less formidable, though in a quite different way, were the foes within.

Gnosticism had not laid down its arms. On the contrary, it was in the middle of this century that its most virulent champion appeared: Marcion, another man from the east, who had settled in Rome. Obsessed with the problem of evil and exaggerating the differences between the Old and New Testaments, he taught that creation is the work of an evil god, the demiurge. As interpreter of the true, good God, he retained only parts of the New Testament The true, good God willed to save the world by sending it his Son, incarnate in Jesus Christ, whom men put to death; but the virtue of this death saves only a part of them, an élite who are able to profit by the salvation thus offered. It is surprising that a doctrine so inhuman and so dishonouring to the gift of God should have had as much success as it did, still more so when we realize that Marcion imposed the strictest asceticism on his followers. But that is the fact: by the end of the second century Marcionism had penetrated almost all the provinces of the empire and almost everywhere threatened the Church. It retained its followers for a long time, though gradually altering its nature.

A very different affair was Montanism, a movement of visionaries, whose founder Montanus, another Asiatic, a native of Phrygia, preached the coming of the Holy Ghost, calling himself his incarnation, or at least his organ. He was supported by two fanatical women, Priscilla and Maximilla, who spread their teachings along with him and preached rigorous practices, to which they soon added new austerities, such as the prohibition of flight in time of persecution and the exclusion of sinners from all penance. The bishops of the Asiatic provinces condemned these excesses, but were not able to check their propagation, and excommunications abounded. Pope Zephyrinus was also obliged to expel these fanatics from the Church, though the gentle Irenaeus of Lyons, always inclined to irenic efforts, as if predestined to them by his name, had hoped to regain them by gentleness and patience. What was at stake was the survival of the Church (the true depositary of a message whose purity was maintained by its hierarchy), now threatened by a spurious Church of prophets, which would have been abandoned, both in its teachings and in the succession of its pastors, to the wildest inspirations of individuals. The infection won over some illustrious Christians, like Tertullian, who was one of the greatest Christian apologists of the second century. It had its followers for many years and had not totally disappeared when the Roman empire fell.

This was not all. The Church had to suffer the assaults

of those who had left her communion and proceeded to attack her essential belief in God himself and her Saviour; but while resisting her rebellious or presumptuous sons she had also to face internal difficulties, about the celebration of her mysteries, on which differences of opinion arose which came to open opposition. The question of the date of Easter nearly provoked a conflict between East and West. In the greater part of the East it had been the custom, appealing to the tradition of St John, to celebrate the feast on the actual day on which our Lord had died, corresponding to the fourteenth day of the Jewish month Nisan. The West, on the contrary, led by Rome, which appealed to St Peter and St Paul, commemorated the day of the Lord's resurrection.[2]

About the middle of the second century St Polycarp of Smyrna, in spite of his years, made the journey to Rome in the hope of achieving unity on this point. But neither he nor Pope Anicetus was able to persuade the other to give up liturgical traditions so deeply rooted. The divergence was serious, however, for the Asiatics, with their custom, seemed not to celebrate the resurrection. Pope Victor (189-99), an African by birth and a man of initiative and resolution, with a vivid consciousness of the universal rôle of the bishop of Rome, felt that the divergence must be ended. In order that the general feeling of the Church might be thoroughly expressed on the subject he urged the convening of meetings of bishops or provincial synods, all of which, except those of Asia Minor, decided for the western tradition. The Asiatics being unwilling to yield, Victor decided to excommunicate them. A measure so severe, striking at Churches of such venerable authority, which then formed one of the chief centres of Christianity, provoked some heated reaction, and

[2] Another explanation of this difference is offered by N. M. Denis-Boulet, *The Christian Calendar,* in this series, p. 41.

several bishops, while not disputing Victor's authority, protested to him. Irenaeus, once again playing the part of peacemaker, still remembered in the collect for his feast, proclaimed that it was necessary to follow the Roman custom of celebrating the mystery of the Lord's resurrection on Sunday, but respectfully urged Victor not to excommunicate whole communities for their loyalty to an ancient tradition. Though there are differences in the observance, he said, the faith is the same. This respectful plea was accepted. But the Asiatics adopted the general custom at a time and under conditions which are unknown to us; we may presume therefore that when the time came the agreement was effected without difficulties or disturbance.

CONTEMPORARY DOCUMENTS

IRENAEUS OF LYONS († *about* 202)

A prayer to God

I call upon thee, O Lord, God of Abraham, God of Isaac, God of Jacob and Israel, thou who art the Father of our Lord Jesus Christ, who in thy infinite mercy hast been pleased that we should know thee; thou hast made heaven and earth, thou art the sovereign Lord of all things, thou only art the true God, and there is none higher than thee.

Through our Lord Jesus Christ and the gifts of the Holy Spirit, grant that all my readers may know thee, for thou only art God; confirm them in thee, turn them away from every heretical and impious doctrine which knows not God.

Prayer for the conversion of heretics

For our part, we pray that they [the heretics] may not lie in the pit they have digged for themselves; that they may not depart from their Mother, that they may leave the Abyss, forsake the Void and flee the Ogdoad; that being converted to the Church of God they may be lawfully begotten, and that Christ may be formed in them. May they acknowledge the only true God and Lord of all things as the sole Creator and Fashioner of this world. That is the desire of our charity; offered to God, our love is of more avail than that with which they think they love themselves, and being sincere it will be effective, if only they respond to it. It is like a bitter medicine: it cuts away the dead flesh of the wound, it unmasks their pride and boastfulness. Earnestly and untiringly, then, let us try to stretch out our hands to them. In our next book we intend to present the words of the Lord; may these convince them and draw them away from all error and blashphemy concerning their Creator, who alone is the true God and the Father of our Lord, Jesus Christ. Amen.

THE DIDACHE

(In 1873 a manuscript was discovered called the *Didache* or *Doctrine of the Twelve Apostles*. This anonymous book, highly prized in Christian antiquity, had long been lost. Apparently of Syrian origin, it is a sort of catechism for the use of the faithful, and had an influence on later liturgical documents, especially the Apostolic Constitutions. The prayers which follow were used in the Eucharistic liturgy. They address God as Father and draw their inspiration from the New Testament.)

Eucharistic prayers

As to the Eucharist, give thanks thus; first, concerning the cup:

"We give thee thanks, our Father, for the holy vine of David, thy servant, which thou hast made known to us through Jesus, thy servant. To thee be the glory for evermore."

Next, concerning the broken bread:

"We give thee thanks, our Father, for the life and knowledge which thou hast made known to us through Jesus, thy servant. To thee be the glory for evermore.

"As this broken bread was scattered over the hills, and then, when gathered, become one mass, so may thy Church be gathered from the ends of the earth into thy kingdom. For thine is the glory and the power through Jesus Christ for evermore."

After you are filled, give thanks thus:

"We give thee thanks, holy Father, for thy holy name which thou hast enshrined in our hearts, and for the knowledge and faith and immortality which thou hast made known to us through Jesus, thy servant. To thee be the glory for evermore.

"Thou, Almighty Lord, hast created all things, to the praise of thy name; thou hast given food and drink for men to enjoy, that they may give thee thanks; but us thou hast enriched with spiritual food and drink and eternal life, through thy servant.

"Above all, we thank thee because thou art mighty. To thee be the glory for evermore.

"Remember, O Lord, thy Church; deliver her from all evil and perfect her in thy love. Assemble her from the four winds, this Church which thou hast sanctified, in thy kingdom which thou hast prepared for her, for thine is the power and the glory for evermore.

"May Grace come, and this world pass away! Hosanna to the God of David! If any one is holy, let him come. If he is not, let him do penance. Marana tha! Amen." (*Didache,* 9, 10.)

CHAPTER IV

THE CHURCH
IN THE THIRD
CENTURY: FERMENT
AND EXPANSION

The second century of the Church's history ended with
internal peace restored and a truce to the assaults she had
so often suffered under the rigorous legislation of the
Roman state. But the Church enjoyed little lasting peace.
This second century of a history which had cost the
Church so much bloodshed had scarcely ended when
persecution broke out again.

But now it had a new character. Hitherto, apart from
the murderous outbreak which perpetuated the memory
of Nero's cruelty, the Christians had been attacked only
if they were denounced as such, which meant that they
were under constant threat, made effective at intervals.
Now the state authorities took the initiative. The emperor
Septimius Severus who, like Commodus, had so far been
favourable, led the way by attacking conversions. Soon
after the year 200, after a visit to the East, probably
alarmed at the rapid spread of Christianity, he decreed
the prohibition of baptism. This edict, if rigorously ap-
plied, could have stopped the propagation of Christianity,
and only failed to do so because its application was

neither lasting nor strict. But it was severe enough to disorganize the catechetical school at Alexandria, which was now becoming celebrated. Its head, St Clement, was obliged to flee; Origen, the best known of his pupils, having bravely tried to re-establish it, was arrested. Though he escaped death, several new converts, instructed by him, were put to death. The persecution reached Africa, where it claimed some glorious victims, including the saints Perpetua and Felicity. Popular passions were again unleashed, in some outbreaks even the cemeteries were desecrated, an example of violence exceptional in the Roman world, where graves were nearly always respected. There were also martyrs, or at least confessors for the faith, in Cappadocia and perhaps in Phrygia, in Rome itself and perhaps in Gaul. Then, after a change of ruler, when Caracalla succeeded Septimius Severus, there was again a truce.

The reign of Alexander Severus, a semi-oriental prince, openminded to all novelties, whose mother had held discussions with Origen, encouraged the relaxation. The emperor even thought to honour Christ in his private chapel, along with Alexander the Great, Orpheus and Abraham. But in 235 the sudden death of the young sovereign at the hands of his soldiers, and his replacement by Maximinus of Thrace, a rough man of barbarian stock, was enough to reverse the situation.

Actually, what Maximinus aimed at was mainly to persecute the supporters of his predecessors, and his hostile measures necessarily included the Christians. But they were the object of a special edict which was aimed directly at the clergy only, and particularly the heads of Churches. Pope Pontianus and Hippolytus, a famous teacher of the Roman Church, were condemned to forced labour in the mines of Sardinia, under which they soon succumbed. Some of the Palestinian clergy were imprisoned. In parts of Asia

Minor, where public disasters had aroused the fanaticism of the pagans, accusations against the Christians were given free rein and, in virtue of the ancient laws still in force, more than one capital sentence was passed.

But throughout the empire as a whole there was not much bloodshed and soon, with another change of reign, persecution again ceased. The emperor Philip (243-9), known from his origins as the Arab, proved so tolerant and even favourable that he acquired the reputation of having been the first Christian emperor, fifty years before Constantine. The reputation is certainly unjustified, since he presided over the great pagan festivities of the Secular Games,[1] and the way in which he came to power by the murder of his predecessor does not say much for the reality of his Christianity. In the latter part of his reign, moreover, something occurred which revealed the hostility always smouldering against the Christians, in a part at least of the empire's population. Stirred up by a visionary or charlatan of Alexandria, "a wicked diviner and evil poet"—so wrote Dionysius, bishop of this great city, with its overflowing, mixed population, always ripe for agitation—there was an abrupt rising against the Christians, many of whom were scourged and stoned. A virgin, Apollonia, had her jaw broken and was then burned alive; Serapion, a cleric, was thrown from the top of his house in a sack. Despite its tragic nature, this sudden attack was an isolated event at this period. It was nonetheless a sign of the violent passions which still stirred among the masses against the followers of Christianity.

No doubt these intermittent explosions are at least partially explained by the growing success of the constant Christian propaganda, for the third century undoubtedly marks a period of great progress for the Church. It is notably the period of expansion.

[1] Games celebrated every 120 years.

Palestine, the cradle of the Church, was not the country in which it spread most rapidly, but from there it won over the Hellenic or Hellenized cities of the neighbouring coastline, Caesarea, Ptolemais, Tyre and Berytus, and spread beyond the Jordan into the distant province of Arabia, where as early as the middle of the third century there was a numerous episcopate. It reached Upper Egypt and Cyrenaica, where there were then five towns with bishops. At the same time the evangelization of northern Syria progressed; it already possessed at least a score of episcopal sees. The preaching of the Gospel had already crossed the frontier of the empire in the strict sense and spread into the little protected kingdom of Edessa, and beyond Edessa to the western provinces of the Parthian kingdom, where Christianity was firmly established by the third century. Some time earlier it had reached Armenia and was firmly settled there by the beginning of the fourth century.

But it was in and from Asia Minor that progress was most startling. Gregory, one of Origen's disciples, evangelized the towns and villages with such success that the extraordinary number of his conversions, together with his miracles, earned for him the name of the Wonderworker. The first Christian communities of the Danubian lands appear about 250, and the number of martyrs in Valerian's persecution—bishops, priests, deacons, ordinary layfolk, land workers, solitaries, virgins and married women—gives us some idea of the importance of the conquests achieved between the Danube and the Adriatic.

In Gaul, though the outbreak of persecution in the reign of Marcus Aurelius had decimated the Church of Lyons, it had not halted the propagation of Christianity. One of its greatest missionaries was St Irenaeus, who did not hesitate to learn what was for him the barbarous language of the Celts in order to gain a hearing from them. An inscription at Autun, attributed to Pectorius, one of the "jewels of Christian epigraphy," and one of the most expressive testimonies to eucharistic belief, reveals that there were fervent Christians in this city, where intellect was held in honour, at the beginning of the third century, if not earlier; other cities, such as Dijon and Langres and even the adjacent region of the Rhine, are believed to have had converts at this time. For a long time, however, there was no bishopric for the whole of Gaul save that of Lyons. Under the stimulus of Rome a movement of evangelization followed, and new sees were founded, the first holders of which were in several cases martyrs, such as St Saturninus at Toulouse and St Dionysius at Paris. It was then that distant Britain saw the arrival of its first missionaries.

In the Spanish peninsula, though the paths followed by the propagation of Christianity are still obscure, its results are not in doubt. By the middle of the third century the number of Spanish bishops was already considerable, and by the end of it there were more than forty.

The Acts of the Martyrs, such as those of Sts Perpetua and Felicity, show that in Africa there was already a very complete ecclesiastical hierarchy about the year 200; seventy bishops met in council under their head, the bishop of Carthage, and less than fifty years later a meeting of the same sort mustered eighty-six.

Central Italy did not lag behind. Although at the beginning of the third century there were only three great episcopal sees in Italy outside Rome—Milan, Ravenna and Aquileia—the number was soon doubled for northern Italy, and progress in the peninsula was such that Pope Cornelius presided over a synod of sixty bishops. A letter of his indicates that his own Church comprised forty-six priests, seven deacons, seven subdeacons, forty-two acolytes, fifty-two exorcists, readers and doorkeepers, more than five hundred widows and needy, enabling us to estimate the total Christian population of the capital at some forty thousand souls.

But, so far as we can deduce from the number of Christian inscriptions, the number of martyrs and the strength of pagan reaction, these figures are much lower than those of the East, where already in some places the Christians were not far from being the majority. But without exception the country districts were still scarcely touched, and the very word "pagan," which originally meant a countryman, preserves the memory of this state of affairs.

To balance this, the frontiers of the empire had already been crossed at more than one point. While the empire in general had very little curiosity about what existed beyond these frontiers, Christians, obedient to their Master's express command, had from the first days always been concerned about this larger world. Christianity has been missionary in principle from the outset, and has never ceased to be so. There is known to have been an embryo Church in Persia in the first century, but this only really emerged from obscurity in the third century, during which it spread in this great kingdom, rival to the Roman empire. Its capital, the great city of Seleucia Ctesiphon, was an episcopal see by the end of the century, but already it was not the only one. Georgia and Armenia were also deeply penetrated when the baptism of King Tiridates and his family, about the year 300, gave a fresh impulse to the work of conversion.

Evangelization extended even to India, or at least its approaches. Although the mission attributed to St Bartholomew or to St Thomas is based only on traditions which are far from authenticated, that of the Sicilian Pantaenus is mentioned by the historian Eusebius, who has preserved so many precious though rather confused memoirs of the Church's early days. He does not enable us to say whether these apostles of India reached only the Yemen, or the Abyssinian kingdom of Axum, or the actual Indian peninsula. But a document about the primitive history of Manicheism, discovered in our time, leaves hardly any doubt that a beginning, at least, was made of the work of evangelizing the nearest Indian territories in the third century, and the Christian communities which the celebrated traveller Cosmas Indicopleustes found in Hindustan in the sixth century seem thus to date back to a period before the end of the persecutions in the Roman empire. The Danube too was crossed by the pioneers of the religion which no frontier could halt: the first Churches of the land of the Goths were founded in what is now southern Russia and particularly the Crimea, while in the south of Roman Africa, as in Egypt, the borders of Nubia and the Sahara heard, or were soon to hear, the message of Christ.

So powerful a movement, which strove unceasingly in the heart of the Roman empire for the conquest of hearts and minds, was bound to alarm a power which had always seen in Christianity an enemy or at least a danger. The persecution of Septimius Severus had very soon subsided; that of Maximinus had been a bloody but brief episode; then Philip the Arab, whose cognomen shows him to have been emancipated from Roman traditions, had given the Church such marks of sympathy that he was mistaken by some for one of its members. But once again there was an abrupt reversal. With the emperor Decius, who succeeded Philip in 249, a representative of the old Roman spirit mounted the throne. One of his essential aims was to restore the ancient customs; it was practically inevitable that he should harry the Christians.

With him, persecution for the first time becomes really general and aims at the extermination of Christianity. It is a duel between the Church and the Roman empire.

Decius' edict of persecution compelled all the inhabitants of the empire, or at least all who might be suspected of Christianity, to make an act of adherence to pagan worship, to reverence the emperor's statue, for instance, or to burn a grain of incense before it. A certificate, called a *libellus,* furnished proof of obedience. Refusal was punishable with death. But the magistrates were less anxious to punish disobedience than to obtain obedience, for which all means, from torture to bribes, were employed. "The judges are upset," said Origen, "if torments are supported with courage, but their joy is boundless when they are able to triumph over a Christian." Their object was to make, not martyrs, but apostates, and at first these were very numerous, for Christian courage had become relaxed during the half-century when the blows of persecution had been so few. There were also many who were prepared to obtain their freedom from molestation by buying certificates of conformity, *libelli,* which protected them from molestation. The question of these *libellatici,* whether penance was to be imposed on them, or refused, or deferred, raised delicate problems, the aftereffects of which long agitated the Christian communities. But though the persecution, in spite of defections, had time to claim many victims, it was relatively short, as we have said, and the Church, on which the heroism of the martyrs acted once more as a stimulus, emerged all the stronger.

There was another result: the atrocities ordered by Decius aroused a feeling of pity and disgust at bloodshed among the Roman public. The feeling was no doubt liable to reaction, but public opinion began to change.

But in parts of the Church the persecution produced

lamentable after-effects. Even before it had ended, the
lapsed or the *libellatici* who had repented demanded to
be restored to the Church, and the confessors of the faith,
those who had faced death but escaped it, paradoxically
supported the demands of these weaker brethren and, dis-
regarding the ecclesiastical hierarchy, granted them letters
of pardon, dispensing them from penance. It took all the
firmness of that great bishop of Carthage, St Cyprian, to
check the excessive indulgence of this unnatural alliance
of the brave and the cowards. But the rebels formed a
schism, led by a priest, Novatus. In Rome, on the other
hand, the rigorists, led by the priest Novatian, refused
any pardon to the penitent, and another equally paradoxi-
cal combination was formed, of both Novatus and Novatian, of laxity and rigorism, against both Pope Cornelius
at Rome and Cyprian at Carthage. But the schism of
Novatian was the more serious: it won supporters in
almost all parts of the Church and retained them long
after the persecutions had ended.

But these did not end with the brief but brutal on-
slaught of Decius. The peace which followed it was short.
Less than ten years later the emperor Valerian tried to
put a final stop to Christian life throughout the empire.
Religious meetings were forbidden on pain of death, or
other punishments legally equivalent, such as forced labour in the mines. The first victims were naturally the
heads of the Churches: Pope Sixtus II at Rome, his chief
deacon Laurence and others, the bishop St Cyprian at
Carthage, the deacon James and the reader Marianus at
Cirta (Constantine), the bishop Quadratus and all his
clergy at Utica, the bishop Fructuosus and his deacons at
Tarragona in Spain, the bishops Patroclus at Troyes and
Dionysius at Paris. But many others perished in Africa
and Asia, and even a child like Cyril in Cappadocia. The
terrible catastrophe which ended the reign of Valerian,

treacherously captured by King Sapor of Persia, also ended the persecution. His son Gallienus, whose opinions were quite different from his father's, ordered prosecutions to cease and even restored the churches and cemeteries which Valerian had caused to be confiscated, confirming this measure by granting the heads of the Churches the free exercise of their functions. Not only did the Church again begin to breathe in peace, but it enjoyed half a century of complete freedom and expansion.

Its organization, already in possession of all its essential elements at the beginning of the century, and continually growing stronger, was clearly apparent at the end of it, still true to itself in its strength and simplicity, but with enrichments prompted by its very development.

The bishop was still almost everything in the Church of the third century, but the rôle of the priests began to increase. The growth of the Christian population in the big towns made it necessary to create more ecclesiastical centres, which later came to be called parishes. The first deacon, later to be called the archdeacon, acquired a position of the first importance, owing to the development of the Christian community and the temporal administration resulting from it, and this position tended to make him the chief personage in the community after the bishop, whom he often succeeded. He was given assistants, called subdeacons, and others under them; acolytes, their immediate subordinates; exorcists, whose duty was to deliver those possessed by devils; readers, charged with reading the Scriptures in public and sometimes with the care of the places of worship.

In some regions, where the Christian population outside the city was not yet large enough to need permanent ecclesiastical centres, visiting priests (*periodeutae*) were charged with supplying the needs of these scattered Christians. But in other countries, where the Christian population had probably grown more quickly, the number of bishops multiplied rapidly, which accounts for the impressive figures of those taking part in Italian and African councils of the third century.

The heads of those Churches whose missionary spirit had chiefly contributed to the foundation of others retained a sort of preeminence over them, and those of the great cities, who were as mothers to their daughter-churches, were accepted as heads of the episcopate of a definite region, like Rome in Italy or Carthage in Africa. But on the whole the dominant idea or sentiment in the third century was of a brotherhood of Churches rather than a hierarchical order among them. Still their relations required some sort of regulation in order to preserve and express their unity. Gatherings of bishops in councils or synods, deliberating in common on questions which concerned the whole Church or a great part of it, were one of the spontaneous forms in which this unity was manifested and ensured.

Gradually, however, the most important Church of a province, usually that of the capital or metropolis, tended to assume the lead, and this prepared the way for the institution of metropolitans. The bishoprics of the still more important centres, such as Alexandria in Egypt, Antioch in Asia and Rome in Italy, which were also the Churches most anciently founded, by the apostles or contemporaneously with them, were bound to hold yet higher positions, and this position was wholly exceptional in the case of Rome, which had been the scene of the apostolic missions of both St Peter and St Paul.

As early as about the year 200, the attitude of Pope Victor over the Paschal dispute had shown the head of the Church in Rome to be conscious of a special mission, which he discharged with striking firmness. His two im-

mediate successors, Zephyrinus and Callistus, had to decide their position in the debates aroused by the doctrine
of the Logos, whom it was necessary to maintain as a
distinct Person in the divine Trinity, neither dividing the
Trinity nor making the Son an inferior deity who would
not be truly God. The priest Hippolytus the first Roman
cleric to write a theological work, decided in the second
sense, and Zephyrinus and Callistus refused to follow him.
Hippolytus founded a schism, but returned to the fold at
the end of his life. Callistus also encountered difficulties
with intransigent Christians like the vehement Tertullian;
they regarded Callistus as too indulgent to sinners and
separated from the Roman Church after the publication
of what was called the Edict of Callistus on penitential
discipline, regarded by them as too lenient. But this did
not prevent the authority and prestige of the Roman See
from remaining unrivalled throughout the third century.
Pope Cornelius supported St Cyprian of Carthage with all
his might against the African partisans of laxity, and he
himself was upheld by Cyprian against the contrary attacks of the extreme rigorists. It is that Cyprian and
Cornelius were ranged on opposite sides in a dispute over
the baptism given by heretics, which Rome and almost the
whole Church did not repeat, while Cyprian and his Afri-
cans, like some Asiatics, repeated it. But on this point too,
though the quarrel was fierce at first, agreement came
with the general acceptance of the Roman rule.

Besides this, throughout the course of the third century,
a series of diverse but always significant events proves
the unique place held by the Roman See in the eyes of the
Church in general. There were the visits to Rome of the
most eminent men of the Christian world, like Tertullian
or Irenaeus, but also of heretics like Marcion, who could
not be indifferent to Roman opinion; the numerous letters
from the Roman Church to other Churches on points of

doctrine or discipline, such as those of Victor or Cornelius, testifying to the solicitude of the Roman Church for
the whole Church, as well as for the prestige of Rome, a
prestige independent of the personal qualities of the popes,
for it benefits the office, not the person. The authority of
the bishop of Rome does not derive from his personal
merits, as with Cyprian of Carthage, but from the tradition he embodies. Of course in those early days this authority was rather practised than thought out, more felt
than defined, felt by the Roman pontiffs themselves, felt
also by the others, unless the feeling happened to be
counteracted by some accidental considerations, as in the
case of fixing the date of Easter or the baptism of heretics.
This position was one the pagans themselves realized. In
the reign of the emperor Aurelian, in 270, there were two
rival claimants for the great episcopal see of Antioch and
the civil power had to decide about the property of the
Church; Aurelian had no hesitation in deciding that the
legitimate owner must be the one in communion with the
bishop of Rome.

But this authority of the Church, already so firmly
planted, strong and conscious of itself, underwent some
attacks. Though the Church made magnificent progress in
the third century, it also passed through more than one
crisis. Neither then nor ever, in fact, has the Church been
at rest. The question of the divine Logos, which had become a subject of speculation for the new science of
theology, and the question of penitential discipline, which
was inevitably raised by the frailties of human nature
amid the temptations of everyday life as well as by the
formidable trials of persecution, brought many difficulties
in their train. Heresies and schisms never ceased to appear.

But it was about the middle of the third century that
the most serious doctrinal opposition to the Church arose

in the shape of Manicheism: no mere heresy this time, but a radically hostile doctrine, though it claimed to be handing on the teaching of Jesus.

Its founder was Mani, a native of Persia, where he settled after a journey to India. He aimed at accomplishing a synthesis of Christianity, Buddhism and the Persian religion of Zoroaster, and taught that this synthesis was destined to win the spiritual lordship of the whole world, East and West. Going beyond Marcionism, he professed a radical dualism: the principles of good and evil are eternal, and eternally at war. Matter, the product of the evil principle, is fundamentally evil. The body is therefore evil, and so is the whole process of generation. For those who would be perfect, marriage is forbidden. On the other hand, for those who are content to remain plain "hearers" or catechumens, a wide liberty in the moral sphere is at least implicitly allowed, and this liberty may at least partially explain the great success of the doctrine, though its theoretical rigorism may have attracted other souls, enamoured of purity. Its followers called themselves the pure, *katharoi,* and the name of Cathari, which they long bore, preserved the memory of this aspiration far into the Middle Ages.

The Church's reaction was naturally extremely vigorous, and it was matched by the attitude of the Roman state, which could not be blind to the social perils of the Manichean propaganda. But this did not prevent the latter from making very extensive conquests, though those whom it converted were repeatedly prosecuted and condemned, even to death, and though the Church, in her own sphere, waged a regular crusade against its books. The East was infected by it as far as China: the West was deeply penetrated, as was Africa, where the future St Augustine was seduced in his youth. In the Middle Ages Europe witnessed a revival of Manicheism in the Albigenses and who would dare to say that even today there are no traces of an unconscious Manichean infection, among certain Christians who have a sort of horror of matter, a horror not derived from the Gospel?

But if the Church of Christ, attacked from without and menaced from within, never enjoys calm, neither does she ever lack champions to maintain the purity of her doctrine and win back the dissidents to unity. The dangers of perversion of the authentic teaching of Christ culminated in the third century with the outburst of Manicheism, but this is the century in which a succession of great apologists for the faith—Tertullian and St Cyprian in Africa, St Clement of Alexandria, already active in 200, Origen in Egypt and then in Syria—replied with renewed vigour to the attacks, redressed the deviations of heresy and showed that the teachings of Christ could be translated into the language of human speculation, yet could never itself be mere speculation.

Tertullian was probably born at Carthage, of heathen parents, but was converted and ordained priest. After serious studies in law, he put his very considerable talents at the service of the faith, using them intrepidly in its defence against the injustice of the persecution it was suffering. In various treatises, such as the *Apologeticum, Ad Nationes,* and the book *Adversus Judaeos,* he demonstrates the illogicality of laws which punish, when it is denounced, a supposed crime, which yet must not be sought out, and shows that his brethren, so wrongly accused of atheism and lèse-majesty, because they do not practise the official religion, are the most devoted servants of the state which rejects them, because they are the most obedient to the moral law. An impassioned controversialist, instinctively practising attack as the best form of defence, he grapples with all the heresies of his time, all the known forms of Gnosticism and above all of Marcionism. He maintains the full value of tradition, but his theology is still imperfectly grounded, and the inferiority he attributes to the Son with respect to the Father has led to his being ranked, in our days, among the heretics. It is perhaps as a moralist that he is most to be admired, for the lofty and pure ideals he always sets before his readers, since he is always urging them that the only end worth pursuit is the imitation of God, the imitation of Christ. But led astray by his extremist temperament, the Christian apologist ended in heresy.

In St Cyprian of Carthage we find only rectitude, ardent love for the Church without attachment to personal feeling, and a sense of what is needed for the government of souls. He did, of course, oppose Rome about the rebaptism of heretics, but he did not go the length of an irreparable breach, nor was he alone in his opposition, since Africa and part of Roman Asia were on his side. But what always dominated his thought and regulated his conduct as a bishop was his sense of the unity of the Church, which moved him to write the book with this very title, *De Unitate Ecclesiae;* in point of fact this is not so much a theological treatise as an urgent exhortation to his flock to resist those who would rend this unity. Of this unity, the bishops are the guardians; every bishop ensures it in his own diocese, the episcopal college in the Church as a whole. It is true that if differences appear, some authority is necessary to compose them. It is here that the bishop of Rome has a rôle of primary importance, which Cyprian admitted, teaching that the Chair of Peter is the *ecclesia principalis,* the source and centre of Catholic unity. He did not realize the logical consequence of this admission, the power, namely, pertaining to the bishop of Rome, to impose irreformable decisions, whether doctrinal or disciplinary. This consequence was only to be perceived later. But the whole of Cyprian's preaching was devoted to the exaltation of unity, not only by his writings but by his life which he laid down for the Church in Valerian's persecution in 257, with calm courage, devoid of all ostentation, assisted by his priests and deacons, surrounded by his flock and the respectful silence of the pagans, who now no longer hurled abuse at the condemned bishop, as those of Smyrna had done at the execution of Polycarp a hundred years before. In these hundred years we can see how immense was the ground gained by the Christian faith.

At Alexandria, the chief town of Hellenized Egypt, a cosmopolitan and intellectual city, Christian teachers had very early founded a catechetical school, which had the character of an ecclesiastical institution. It displayed great brilliance under the saintly Clement of Alexandria, a pagan by birth, who in his works the *Protrepticus,* the *Paedagogus* and the *Stromateis,* developed a genuine theological system. It starts with a moral preparation, in which he tries to use the Hellenic philosophers in order to expound the Christian faith, towards which, this moral preparation can guide certain minds; it also helps to defend the faith against those who attack it in the name of the intellect. But faith goes far beyond intellect, for it gives men the knowledge of God revealed by his Word himself. In this knowledge, according to Clement, some make greater progress because they add to it a deeper knowledge than that obtained by study, a knowledge which Clement calls *gnosis.* The "gnostic," he holds, is superior to the simple believer, as gnosis is superior to ordinary faith. The name alone, recalling the earlier heresies, was enough to show the danger of a concept which might well cause faith to be underestimated, and the Church has not accepted these views. But it has not denied Clement's lofty aspirations, any more than the sanctity of his life, so entirely devoted to the service of God's glory.

Surpassing all the others by his influence is Origen, Clement's successor as head of the Alexandrian school, which was forced by persecution to transfer to Alexandria. The supreme interest of his work for modern Christians lies perhaps in its systematic discussion with the pagan intellectuals of his time and in the light it throws on the pagan reaction to Christianity, and the reply to be made to it. But Origen's polemics are not confined to apologetics: the object of his theological work was not merely to refute his opponents but also to instruct the faithful, those at least who were not satisfied with elementary instruction but aspired to a profounder penetration of the truth. Origen put at their disposal an immense knowledge and vast exegetical material. The collection of all his writings, in which he discusses point by point the objections of educated pagans, is a sort of early Christian *Summa,* into which the author has poured his whole self, with his perfect command of the Scriptures, his sense of dogma and a general philosophy of Christianity. He did not shrink from introducing his personal views, some of which could hardly be accepted, such as the pre-existence of souls, their descent into matter and the universal "restoration," that is, the final salvation of all, if not of Satan himself, though he stoutly denied that he had taught this. And so his writings and his preaching, which at the end of his career had become not only daily but almost incessant, exerted an extraordinary influence. This aroused, at least in the East, a sort of enthusiasm, but also, especially in the West, considerable opposition, which after his death caused him to be reckoned among the heretics.

In any case, taking an overall view of the development of Christian thought in the third century, what chiefly strikes us is that while pagan culture, in Hellenic and Roman circles alike, has ceased to produce any works worthy of attention, it is in Christian literature, whether in Rome, Greece, Asia or Africa, that we find men and writings of real worth.

But it is not only intellectual progress which, though never adding to dogma, seems to increase the spiritual wealth of the Church and make it more attractive. As it continually penetrates the world, its hold on it becomes also more visible.

The Church in this period is certainly no longer a hidden Church. It used to be thought that it was only able to live and grow, in spite of the laws against it, by disguising itself under cover of associations which were legal or at least tolerated, like those called "colleges" or clubs of common people, of which the associations for burial purposes were typical. The reality was very different. The Christian Church, as a society, was known to the civil authorities at a very early date, certainly before the third century. It was known as such in the members who composed it, chiefly in the persons of its heads; if a persecution broke out the imperial police knew where to lay their hands on them. It was known as such, too, in its property, which it had already begun to possess. In the earliest days there had been no ecclesiastical property apart from the property of individual Christians, of such, that is, who had any, and put their private houses at the disposal of the community for the celebration of the mysteries, just as they granted to some or other of their brethren the use of their family burial-places in which to bury their dead. But little by little things changed. While the use of family cemeteries and private houses for worship does not totally disappear, corporate ecclesiastical property is an institution in the third century. There are cemeteries belonging to the Christian communities and there are churches for the Christians' religious meetings. In these precautions are taken, no doubt, against too much publicity; the sacred character of the Christian mysteries is opposed to it, according to the "discipline of the secret," as it has been called, which does not display to the public gaze what calls for reverence; but there is no attempt to prevent its being known.

Nor did the Christians live, as has sometimes been imagined, in those underground cemeteries, the catacombs, nor were they always forced to hide their life of worship in them. This clandestine worship is typical only of the periods of intense persecution. At other times they went down to the catacombs only to commemorate the martyrs or confessors who were buried there, and moreover it was only after the peace of the Church that this cult became general. But in the third century, perhaps even at the end of the second, they began to adorn the vaults and walls of the catacombs with paintings, usually symbolical, in which there appear the *orante* (a female figure at prayer), the anchor and the Tau (T), recalling while disguising the cross, the symbol of death, which were the beginnings of Christian art. These are so many evidences of a faith which seeks to express itself before the faithful while still not betraying itself openly to those outside. But while belief does not make a display of itself, for the sacred must always preserve its mystery, the believers are not men who hide themselves. Third century Christendom lives in the open. And yet, Christianity was still prohibited in theory; no imperial rescript ever recognized it as a *religio licita,* or pronounced the Christian communities to be authorized associations. The legal restrictions were still there. But it became increasingly impossible to take them seriously. The marvellous luxuriance of the Lord's Vine burst asunder all bonds.

Yet an outbreak of hostility always remained possible. The threat never ceased to menace the followers of Christ, and sometimes it was put into effect, with terrible cruelty, as under Decius or Valerian. And so the prospect of martyrdom was always present to Christian hearts. One of Origen's treatises is called the *Exhortation to Martyrdom,* and although from his time to the end of the century things continued to develop in the direction of a lasting peace, this peace was undeniably precarious.

But during the fifty years after Valerian's persecution the Church enjoyed a period of almost complete peace, and Christianity and its teachings penetrated still deeper into the Roman world. These teachings were given and and repeated by means of the spoken word and sometimes by the writings of the Christians, such as the apologists, and bishops like Cyprian, but their example alone was already a powerful persuasive. The Christian, then as earlier, was one to whom the commands of a higher morality dictated a manner of life which distinguished him from his fellow-citizens, without segregating him from the community. The prescriptions of Christian morality restricted his participation in civic life by forbidding him all overt acquiescence in pagan worship; this alone obviously barred him from many of the ceremonies associated with public life, but his participation in civic life was nonetheless real. If it was not universal, nor certainly the same everywhere, we have knowledge of its manifestations, by precise evidence, from one end of the empire to the other. In its two extremities of Spain and Asia, we see Christians performing municipal functions: in Spain, the Council of Elvira, where rigorism is apparent, forbids the presidents of the local governments to attend church, but only during their year of office, when contact with acts of pagan worship was doubtless difficult to avoid altogether, but participation in the municipal administration is not forbidden. The functions of the imperial Court were also open to Christians, who were then dispensed by the emperor's goodwill (so long as this prevailed) from attendance at pagan ceremonies.

Christians were faced, however, with a grave problem, that of military service. Of course this was not compulsory for all, apart from exceptional occasions, but it obliged those who joined the army both to shed blood and to accept many contacts with pagan worship. The problem of "conscientious objection" was thus raised by Christian writers. But their declarations against military service were never the teaching of the Church, which, while certainly not encouraging the faithful to enlist, held the defence of one's earthly country to be a duty. There were always Christians in the Roman armies, and while they showed clearly that they were not as others, they did not purposely put themselves outside the state.

Quite definitely, the life of Christians in the state is that of men who, still a tiny band at the beginning of the second century, are now steadily progressing to be a considerable and sometimes imposing minority and even, in some regions, becoming the majority of the population. Being then, by the fact of their increase, more involved in the common life, they bring to it the leaven of a higher idea, capable of making them the best of citizens, but they are inevitably more influenced by contact with it, a contact which is sometimes a contagion. The ideal itself is not lowered, and never was lowered, but the proportion of Christians whose behaviour matches up to it tends perhaps to decrease as their total number increases. The heroic tension of the first two centuries is relaxed, especially during the periods of peace between the persecutions, which are indeed more general and more implacable than in the past, but also more limited in their duration.

In short, even if the spirit of the world does not gain

ground among the Christians, it does at least taint them
a little in proportion as Christianity gains ground in the
world. Some practices thus grow up which would surely
have surprised the faithful of the first two centuries. Men
who are Christians in heart and conviction, but lack the
courage to keep all the obligations of their baptism, prefer
to postpone it. Penance, however, has become more accessible than in the days of primitive Christianity, when
it was something exceptional and very rigorous. Sexual
purity always remained a strict obligation for the faithful,
for whom it is a grave sin to be incontinent outside marriage, but the modification by Pope Callistus of the pen-
ances imposed for these sins is an indication of a more
tolerant morality, practically inevitable with the growth
of the original little flock. It is true that in opposition to
the lukewarm and the feeble there were rigorists, who
endeavoured to propagate a stricter morality than that of
the Gospel, preferring the teachings of the apocryphal
books. We know that the Church never encouraged their
exaggerations, but it did encourage the ascetic practices
of a chosen few, such as continence and voluntary virginity. This chosen few served as an example and a stimulus to the rank and file, who found even the common
morality hard enough. It was natural that the clergy
should be the first to give an example in this field, and it
was thus that what later became the precept of clerical
celibacy began as a practice which was not at first obligatory, but tended to be imposed.

The greater strictness of Christian morality, in contrast
with the license of pagan behaviour, was equally evident
in the sphere of economics. By the end of the third century, of course, it was a far cry from the days when the
first Christians had held their goods in common, but the
moralists of Christian antiquity maintained strict rules in
the matter of acquiring and using material goods. Lending

at interest was universally disapproved by them, no doubt because it was so in the Bible, but also because it could not fulfil the economic functions it does in modern society and because, owing to the abuses actually inherent in it, they did not distinguish it from usury in the strict sense, which for us is characterized by excessive rates of interest. The injunctions of the councils, such as that of Elvira, are proof that disobedience was not exactly rare among the faithful, perhaps even among the clergy, but in this sphere, of course, as in so many others, there were both lax and rigorous opinions.

But there was one point on which Christian doctrine and practice never ceased to be asserted with unequivocal clarity, and that was the obligation of charity. The Christian, because he loves God, must love all men, who are God's children, as his brothers, and whatever failures and slackness there may have been in individual cases, the example never ceased to be given. The impression this charity made on the pagans is well known. But it was not confined to those who shared the same faith, *domestici fidei,* as St Paul calls them, though they might be, as he admits, objects of preference. This charity, which did not stop at feelings but was expressed in deeds, proved itself "ingenious," as the Apostle says again, by inventing, at need, what pagan antiquity had never known, still less produced: hospices for the aged and hospitals for the sick poor and, in a more general way, help for all who were in need. A positively new kind of society, more humane because it was nourished from sources which were divine, was gradually coming into being along with Christianity.

To arrest this development the Roman power made one last, supreme effort.

CONTEMPORARY DOCUMENTS

CHRISTIAN LIFE

(The liturgy of baptism and the eucharistic liturgy from the *Apostolic Tradition;* the *Apostolic Tradition* of Hippolytus is the only liturgical book we possess from the third century.)

Baptism

At cock-crow, the candidates are brought near to pure, running water. The priest takes apart each one who is to receive baptism and bids him renounce, facing the West[1] and saying:

I renounce thee, Satan, and all thy allurements and thy works.

After this declaration he is anointed with the oil of exorcism, with these words: Let all evil spirits depart from thee.

The candidate then goes down into the water and the baptizer lays a hand on his head, saying:

Dost thou believe in God, the Father almighty?

And the one to be baptized answers: I believe.

The baptizer baptizes him once, having his hand laid on his head. Then he says: Dost thou believe in Christ Jesus, the Son of God, who was born of Holy Spirit and the Virgin Mary, died and was buried, rose living from the dead on the third day, ascended into heaven, sat down at the right hand of the Father and will come to judge the living and the dead?

---

[1] The East stands for the direction of Paradise, whence Christ will return: the West for the haunt of devils.

He says: I believe.

And the baptizer baptizes him a second time, and then says: Dost thou believe in the Holy Spirit and in the Holy Church for the resurrection of the flesh?

And the baptized says: I believe.

And he is baptized a third time. When he comes up from the water, a priest gives him the anointing with the consecrated oil, saying:

I anoint thee with the holy oil, in the name of Jesus Christ.

They dry themselves and put on their clothes, then they return to the church.

The bishop lays his hand on them, saying the following invocation:

O Lord God, who hast made thy servants worthy to receive the remission of sins through the washing of regeneration of the Holy Ghost, send thy grace upon them that they may serve thee according to thy will, for to thee is the glory, Father, Son and Holy Ghost, in the Holy Church, now and for the ages of ages. Amen.

He takes the consecrated oil in his hand and anoints them on the head, saying:

I anoint thee with the holy oil in the Lord, the Father almighty, in Christ Jesus and in the Holy Ghost.

After this anointing he gives each a kiss, saying:

The Lord be with you.

The baptized answers: And with thy spirit.

The Anaphora

(The oldest prayer we possess for the consecration of the eucharistic oblations is that of Hippolytus. Addressed to the Father, it does not extend to the benefits of creation but is concentrated, as in baptism, on the mysteries of Christ. It invokes the Holy Spirit on the oblations, the Church and the communicants.

We note the absence of the *Sanctus* which, in later liturgies, breaks the continuity and is suggested by association with the praises of the angelic choirs.)

The bishop, with the whole college of priests,[2] says this prayer of thanks:
The Lord be with you.
And all answer:
And with thy spirit.
Let us lift up our hearts
They are with the Lord.
Let us give thanks unto the Lord.
It is meet and right.
And he continues:
We give thee thanks, O God, through thy beloved Child Jesus Christ, whom in the last times thou didst send to us, a Saviour and Redeemer and Messenger of thy counsel; who is thy inseparable Word, through whom thou madest all things, and in whom thou wast well pleased. Thou didst send him from heaven into a Virgin's womb, he was conceived and was made flesh, and was shown to be thy Son, being born of Holy Spirit and a Virgin; who, fulfilling thy will and acquiring a holy people for thee, stretched forth his hands for suffering, that he might free from suffering those who believed in thee. And when he was betrayed to voluntary suffering, that he might abolish death and rend the bonds of the devil and tread underfoot hell, and enlighten the righteous, establish the ordinance and demonstrate his resurrection, taking bread and giving thanks, he said: Take, eat, this is my Body which is broken for you, Likewise also for the cup, he said: This is my Blood which is shed for you: when you do this, do it for my memorial.

[2] Clearly we have here a concelebration, that is, a joint and single celebration by the bishop and his priests, at Rome. St Cyprian records the use of the same formulas, in Africa (*On the Lord's Prayer,* 31).

Doing, therefore, the memorial of his death and resurrection, we offer to thee the bread and the cup, giving thanks to thee because thou hast found us worthy to stand before thee and minister unto thee: and we beseech thee that thou wouldst send thy Holy Spirit upon this oblation of thy Holy Church, to join together in unity all those who partake, to fill them with the Holy Spirit, to confirm their faith in the truth, that we may praise and glorify thee through thy Child Jesus Christ; through whom glory and honour be to thee, to Father and Son, with the Holy Spirit, in thy Holy Church, now and for ever and world without end. Amen.

CHRISTIAN PRAYER

As soon as they wake in the morning, before they do anything else, let all the faithful, men and women, wash their hands and pray to God, and then let them go about their business.

But if there should be any instruction, let them give it the preference, being inwardly assured that it is God who speaks by the mouth of the instructor. Whoever has prayed thus in the assembly of the brethren is forearmed against the evils of the day. A man who fears God should feel it a great loss to miss the instruction, especially if he knows how to read.

When the instructor is there, all must hasten to the meetingplace where the instruction takes place. He who speaks will be given grace to speak things profitable for all. You will hear things you did not think to hear, and you will profit by what the Spirit says to you by the mouth of the speaker. Thus your faith will be strengthened by the words you hear, and he will tell you how you should behave at home. Let everyone, then, be careful to go to the assembly, where the Holy Spirit bestows his fruits . . .

On days when there is no instruction, everyone in his home should take a holy book and read enough to profit his soul.

The hours of prayer

If you are at home, pray at the third hour [*about 9* A.M.] and praise God. If you are elsewhere at that time, pray to God in your heart, for it was at this hour that Christ was nailed to the Cross. For this cause the Law of the Old Testament ordered the loaves of proposition to be offered at this hour, as a type of the Body and Blood of Christ, and bade men sacrifice the non-rational lamb, which prefigured the perfect Lamb. Christ is indeed the Shepherd, as he is the Bread come down from heaven.

Pray likewise at the sixth hour [*at noon*], remembering Christ on the Cross, when the daylight was divided and it became darkness. At that hour be earnest in prayer, imitating him who prayed while the world was made dark for the unbelieving Jews.

At the ninth hour [*3* P.M.] prolong your prayer and praise, in the spirit of the just praising God who lieth not, who remembered his saints and sent them his Word to bring them light. At this hour Christ shed forth water and blood from his opened side; he gave light to the close of that day, until the evening, and by causing the light to return at the same time as his falling asleep, he gave a type of his resurrection.

Pray also before your body takes its rest. At midnight, rise and wash your hands in water and pray. If your wife is with you, pray together. If she is not yet a Christian, withdraw into another room to pray, then return to your bed.

Be not slothful to pray. He who is married is not thereby defiled. "A man who has bathed does not need to do more than wash his feet; he is clean all over."

(John 13. 10.) When you sign yourself with your moist breath, by catching your breath in your hand, your body is pure all over, down to the feet. For the gift of the Spirit and the rite of the blessed water, welling up as from a spring, drawn from a heart full of faith, have purified the believer.

We must, then, pray at this hour, because our fathers, from whom we have received this tradition, have taught us that the whole creation then rests for a moment, to praise the Lord. The stars, the plants and the waters stand still for a moment, and the whole choir of angels joins with the souls of the just to sing the praises of God. Therefore the faithful too should be careful to pray at that hour. Our Lord himself testifies to it, saying: "Behold the bridegroom is on his way; go out to meet him." (Matt. 26. 6.) And he adds: "Be on the watch; the day of it and the hour of it are unknown to you" (Matt. 25. 13).

At cockcrow, rise again and do the same. At that hour, when the cock crowed, the children of Israel denied Christ, whom we have known by faith; we await the day of the resurrection of the dead, in the hope of eternal light.

If you act thus, all you who are faithful, and make memorial of these mysteries, instructing one another in them and giving an example of them to the catechumens, you will never fall into temptation or lose your souls, since you will always be mindful of Christ.

On the Sign of the Cross

Do your best at all times to make the sign of the Cross on your forehead worthily. This sign of the Passion is a tried remedy against the devil, provided you make it in the spirit of faith and not to be seen of men, knowing that you are thus protecting yourself as with a shield.

When the Adversary sees the inner power thus outwardly displayed, showing our likeness to the Word, he takes to flight; not that he is afraid of you, but because of the Spirit which breathes in you. Moses sacrificed a lamb and sprinkled the lintels and doorposts with its blood, signifying the faith we now have in the Paschal Lamb. So let us sign ourselves on the forehead and the eyes with our hand, to drive away him who seeks to destroy us. (Hippolytus, *Apostolic Tradition.*)

EUCHARISTIC INVOCATION

The funerary inscription of Pectorius of Autum (early third century)

(*Note:* the Greek word *Ichthus,* meaning fish, is composed of the initial letters of the Greek words for "Jesus Christ, Son of God, Saviour." The fish was thus a symbol of Christ.)

Divine race of the heavenly *Ichthus,*
Receive with reverential hearts
Immortal life given to mortals.
Friend, let thy soul renew its youth in the divine waters,
Through the eternal waves of the treasure-giving wisdom.
Receive the honey-sweet food of the Saviour of the saints,
Assuage thy hunger, quench thy thirst; thou holdest
The *Ichthus* in the palms of thy hands.
Feed us, then, Master and Saviour, with the *Ichthus.*

Light of the dead, I pray thee that my mother may rest in
   peace.
And thou, Aschandius my father,
And my sweet mother and my brothers,
With all the thankfulness of my soul I beg you,
In the peace of the *Ichthus,* remember Pectorius.

PRAYERS FROM CYPRIAN OF CARTHAGE
(† 258)

A universal prayer

With sincere hearts and with one accord let us beseech the Lord, with groans and tears let us call upon him, as we must call, who stand between the miserably vanquished, beating their breasts, and the faithful who fear lest they too may yield, between a host of wounded who have fallen and a little band who stand upright. Let us pray that we may soon have peace again, that help may speedily come to scatter our darkness and dangers, that the changes revealed to his servants may be brought about: the restoration of his Church, the assurance of our salvation; after darkness, light; after storms and tempests, a gentle calm.

Let us beg that his fatherly affection may come to our aid, that he may perform the marvels of his power, so that the blasphemies of the persecutors may be confounded, the penance of the fallen may be more regular and the firm and constant faith of those who have persevered may be glorified.

A prayer in litany form

Let us pray for those who have fallen, that they may be raised up.

Let us pray for those who stand, that they may not yield under trial.

Let us pray for those whose fall has been reported, that they may realize how heinous is their offence and understand that no short or light amendment will avail for it.

Let us pray that the pardon granted them may be efficacious and followed by penance,

That they may own their guilt and give proof of their patience by their waiting;

that they may not disturb a still unstable Church,

that they may shrink from provoking persecution within the Church and crowning their guilt by proving unable to keep the peace.

Modesty is what most befits those whose sins spring from dispositions contrary to modesty. Let them knock on the door, not break it down; draw near to the threshold, not cross it; let them mount guard at the gate of the heavenly camp, but with arms of humility, owing thereby that they have been deserters.

Let them sound the trumpet of prayer, but not play boastful tunes. Let them be armed with humility and the shield of faith, which they forsook under fear of death; let them put them on again, armed now against the devil, no longer against the Church, still suffering from their fall. Greatly will they benefit from humble prayer, reverent position, active patience. Let them send their tears to plead for them, let the groans drawn from their breasts be their intercessors, let them give proof of their repentance for the crimes they committed and the shame they feel for them.

Prayer for peace

We pray and beseech God that the enemies of the Church may cease from provoking and plaguing us and may resolve to soften their hearts; may lay aside their anger and return to a peaceful mind; may their hearts, now blinded by the darkness of their sins, perceive the light of penitence, may they ask for the bishop's prayer, not prepare to shed his blood.

Prayer for perseverance

Therefore, since your prayers at this time have the more efficacy, in that prayer is more readily granted in the midst of persecution, earnestly beg the divine mercy that we may all perfectly confess his Name and go forth innocent and glorious from the darkness and snares of this world. United to you in the bonds of charity and peace, standing up together to face the insults of the heretics and the persecutions of the heathen, may we also rejoice with you in the kingdom of God.

PRAYERS FROM CLEMENT OF ALEXANDRIA
(† before 215)

(From the end of the second century there existed a school at Alexandria, under ecclesiastical authority, designed to prepare for baptism young Christians from the most cultivated families of Greek society. Clement and Origen taught in turn in this city, the former privately, the latter in the official school, where he founded courses for higher studies.

Clement, a pagan by birth, combined Hellenic culture with a profound knowledge of the Scriptures. His book the *Paedagogus* was designed to lead the young converts to the school of the one Teacher, Christ. It ends with the famous hymn to Christ, which was perhaps the Alexandrian "School Song" (B. Altaner). It is a hymn full of enthusiasm, inspired by both the Bible and Plato, and preceded by a prayer to the Saviour, in which the final doxology associates the Son with the Father and the Holy Spirit.)

Prayer to the divine Teacher

O Teacher, Father, Guide of Israel, Father and Son both, and Lord, be favourable to thy children. Grant us that by following thy commandments we may attain to the likeness of the Image, and to realize, so far as lies in us, that God is good and not a vindictive judge. Grant us to live in thy peace, to be transported to thy city, crossing without shipwreck the ocean of sin, wafted on by the sweet breeze of the Holy Spirit, who is ineffable Wisdom. Grant us, night and day, until the dawn of the eternal day, to sing to thee a song of thanksgiving. Receive our prayer, O Father and Son, O Son and Father, O Son, our Teacher and Master, with the Holy Spirit.

All to the One, in whom are all things and by whom all are one, by whom is eternity, of whom we are all members, to whom is glory in the ages. All to God who is good, to God who is lovely, to God who is wise, to God who is just! To him be glory, now and for evermore! Amen.

Hymn to Christ the Saviour

Bridle of untamed colts, Wing of the birds in steady flight, strong Rudder of the ships, Shepherd of the royal sheep, gather together the flock of your pure children, that they may praise with holiness and sing with sincerity, with lips without guile, the Christ who leads his children.

Sovereign of the saints, invincible Word of the Father all-high, Prince of wisdom, Support of our labours, eternal Joy: O Jesus, Saviour of our mortal race, Shepherd, Worker, Bridle and Rudder, Wing towards heaven of the company of the saints: Fisher of men whom thou willest to save, on the sea of sin thou dost catch pure fishes; from the menacing wave thou leadest them to the life of bliss. Guide thy flock of the sheep of wisdom; lead, O King, thy children without blame. The footsteps of Christ are the way to heaven.

O God eternal, Age without end, Light immortal, Fountain of mercy, Worker of virtue, Life to be revered of those who sing to God!

O Christ Jesus, thou art the heavenly milk of the sweet breasts of a young bride, of the graces of thy wisdom. We, little children, whose tender mouths quench their thirst from thee, are refreshed in all chastity by the spring of the Spirit.

Let us sing together pure songs, loyal hymns, to Christ our sovereign, sacred prize of the life given by his voice. Let us praise with sincere hearts the Son almighty. Let us who are born of Christ form the choir of peace; people of wisdom, sing all together to the God of peace.

PRAYERS FROM ORIGEN († 253)

(Origen is unquestionably the most representative figure of the School of Alexandria. He was born in that city, his father being a Christian who died a martyr. When still young he was appointed Master of the catechetical school, where his teaching was extremely brilliant. With the finest intellectual qualities he combined a deep faith and a mystical enthusiasm which were to lead him to martyrdom.)

Origen is the greatest theologian of the Greek Church. The subject of controversy during his life and even more after his death, he is now much studied. He combines classical culture with a remarkable knowledge of Scripture, which is always evident, intimately woven into all his writings. He first establishes the critical text of the Bible and then comments on it, drawing out its allegorical or spiritual sense.

Besides his treatise *De Oratione,* his commentaries and homilies conclude with prayer. Prayer flowers naturally from his commentary. It is often addressed to our Lord, with a quite individual note of affective piety and devotion to Christ which is something new, anticipating Bernard of Clairvaux and St Francis of Assisi. Along with much that is obsolete, the essential part of his work is surprisingly relevant. (The following prayers are taken from conclusions to the Homilies.)

Noe's ark and the flood

Let us beseech the mercy of almighty God that he will make us not only hear his word but do it. May he pour over our souls the flood of his waters, that unhindered he may destroy in us all that should be destroyed and revive in us all that should be revived, through Christ our Lord and through his Holy Spirit. To him be the glory in the eternity of the ages! Amen.

The circumcision of Abraham, sign of the Covenant

The Lord grant us to "believe with the heart, to confess with the lips," to show forth with our works, that the Covenant of God is in our flesh, that men may see our good works and glorify our Father in heaven, through Jesus Christ our Lord, to whom glory is due, for ever and ever! Amen.

Agar's eyes are opened

Let us then be wakeful and say with the prophet: Never shall these eyes have sleep, these eye-lids close, until I have found the Lord a home, the great God of Jacob a dwelling-place. To him be the glory and the power, to endless ages! Amen.

God says to Jacob: Joseph will put
his hands on your eyes

May the Lord Jesus put his hands on our eyes also, that we may begin to see, not the things which are seen, but the things which are not seen. May he open our eyes, that they may rest not on things present but on the good things to come; may he unveil the eyes of our hearts to behold God in spirit, through the same Lord Jesus Christ, to whom belong glory and power, to endless ages! Amen.

Spiritual Understanding of the Law of God

Let us beseech the Lord, let us beseech the Holy Spirit, that he may be pleased to drive away all clouds and darkness which through our sins might darken our sight: may he give us a wonderful spiritual understanding of the Law, according to the word of him who wrote: Open thou my eyes, and I will consider the wondrous things of thy Law.

Knowledge of the Scriptures

Let us meditate day and night, let us persevere vigilantly in prayer, let us beseech the Lord himself to give us the knowledge of the Scriptures, that we may put it into practice and so merit spiritual grace, enlightened by the law of the Holy Ghost, in Christ Jesus our Lord, to whom are due the glory and the power, to endless ages. Amen.

Spiritual understanding of the Scriptures

Let us ask the Lord to give us a clearer understanding of his other prophecies, to open our eyes yet more fully to the truth, that we may be able to consider in the Spirit what has been written in the Spirit, expounding spiritual things in spiritual terms, according to God and the Holy Spirit, and may teach us to understand what he has inspired, in Christ Jesus our Lord, to whom are due the glory and the power. Amen.

For peace of soul

Let us pray that Jesus may reign over us, that our land may be kept free from war, that we may be freed from the assaults of our carnal lusts and that every man may then rest under his own vine and his fig-tree and his olive.

The soul which has found peace of body and mind rests in the shadow of the Father and the Son and the Holy Spirit. To the eternal God be glory to endless ages! Amen.

Welcoming Jesus

Let us make ready in ourselves a heart without stain, that the Lord Jesus may enter with joy and thanks into the world of our heart and ask hospitality. To him be glory and power to endless ages! Amen.

Faithfulness in trials

Let us pray to God with our whole heart that we may strive to the end, with the might of soul and body, for the truth. If he should please to test our faith even in persecution (for our faith is tested in perils and persecutions as gold in the furnace), may he find us prepared, lest our dwelling fall down in winter, lest our house be swept away by the storm, as if built on the sand. And when we are blown on by the winds of the Devil, the wickedest of spirits, may our works remain, which till now have been held fast—if only they have not been secretly undermined—and may we show forth on our pilgrimage the love which we bear to God in Christ Jesus, to whom is due the glory and the power to endless ages. Amen.

The example of Simeon

Let us too stand in the Temple, let us too take in our arms the Son of God and hold him close; thus may we become worthy to be let freely depart in peace and to set out for the better joys. Let us pray to the almighty Lord, pray too to the child Jesus himself, whom we long to welcome and clasp in our arms. To him be the glory and empire to endless ages! Amen.

CHRISTIAN DEATH

(What famous martyrs there were at this time! Saints Perpetua and Felicity at Carthage (203), St Apollonia at Alexandria (250) and St Cyprian at Carthage (258) are well known. From many others less well known we choose Montanus and Lucius and their companions, also at Carthage, in 259.)

Letter from the confessors to the
Church at Carthage

We too, beloved brethren, are fighting in your ranks. We are always mindful of the company of our brethren: that is the first duty of the servants of God, who are vowed to the service of Christ.

Guided by these considerations, our love and duty have inspired this letter. Thus we will leave to our brethren after us a faithful witness to the power of God and the record of our toils and trials endured for the Lord.

First of all, the bloodthirsty governor had incited the rioting by the people so as to urge them to massacre. Next day began the terrible persecution of the Christians. Finally the magistrate caused us to be brutally arrested: Lucius, Montanus, Flavian, Julian, Victoricus, Primolus, Renus and Donation. The last was still a catechumen: he was baptized in prison and gave up the ghost there and then. He hastened to pass unspotted from the water of baptism to the martyr's crown. Primolus died in the same way. He too had confessed his faith a few months before, and this was his baptism.

We were therefore handed over to the charge of the local magistrates from the time of our arrest, when we had heard the governor's intentions from the soldiers: the day before he had threatened us with the stake, and in fact, as we learned later from a reliable source, he had meant to burn us alive. But the Lord, who alone can preserve his servants from the flames and holds the thoughts and hearts of kings in his hands, saved us from the governor's revolting cruelty. We had prayed constantly with full faith and had quickly obtained what we asked. The flames were already blazing to destroy our bodies when the faggots which had been kindled went out. The Lord's dew had quenched the flames of the fiery furnace. We who believe can readily compare this marvel with those of the past, as the Lord had promised by his Holy Spirit. Of old he had shown forth his power to save the three holy children, and now he triumphed likewise in us.

The governor, thwarted in his design by the restraining hand of the Lord, sent us back to prison. The soldiers took us back there, but the gloomy horror of the place did not terrify us in the least. Soon this dark prison glowed with the brightness of the Spirit. Instead of the phantoms of the dark and the impenetrable veils of night, the fervour of our faith, bright as day, clothed us with dazzling light, and we went up into this dungeon of sorrows as if we were ascending to heaven.

And yet what days we spent there, and what nights! No words can describe it. The torments of the prison are unspeakable. We are in no danger of exaggerating the horror of this dungeon, for the greater the trial, the greater is he who overcomes it in us. When the Lord is helping us, it is no battle but a victory. For the servants of God, to be killed is a small thing: death is nothing, for the Lord has blunted its edge and conquered its violence by the triumph of the Cross. Besides, it is only for a soldier that we speak of arms, and one is armed only for a battle. Our crowns are won only by a contest and the palm is not awarded till after the battle.

At last, after some days, we were encouraged by the visit of our brethren. All the sufferings of the night vanished before the comfort and joy of the day.

About this time, Renus, one of our company, had a dream in his sleep. He saw men being led out to die, advancing one by one, and before each one a lamp was carried. Those before whom no lamp was carried did not go on to the end. He saw us all pass by with our lamps, and then he woke up. When he told us this dream we were overjoyed, for we were sure that now we would walk with Christ, who is the light of our steps and the Word of God.

This night was followed by a day spent all in joy. On this same day we were taken before the procurator, who had replaced the late consul. O day of joy! Glory of the confessors in chains! O chains, object of all our desires! O irons, more exquisite and precious than purest gold! O music of iron clashing on iron!

Our comfort lay in speaking of our approaching fate. Our only fear was that our happiness might be delayed. Our soldiers did not know where the governor wished to hear us and they led us hither and thither round the whole forum. At last the governor had us called into the audience-chamber, but the hour of our passion was not yet. We emerged victors from this encounter, in which we had vanquished the devil, and were led back to prison, being reserved for another victory.

Beaten in this contest, the devil contrived other devices: he tried to prove us by hunger and thirst, and repeated this attack for many days, thinking these tactics would be more effective. Reduced to the prison skilly and cold water, many of us fell ill.

These sufferings, privations and times of misery, all these, dear brethren, came from God, for wishing thus to prove us he spoke to us in the midst of our trials, in a

vision. It was Victor the priest, our companion in martyrdom, who had this vision, but he died soon after it.

He saw a child, he said, coming into the prison, his
face shining with indescribable light. This child led us
about everywhere to take us out, but without success.
Then he said to Victor, "You have still to suffer some
more, for you are being detained. Trust me, I am with
you," and he added: "Tell your companions that your
crown will be the more glorious. The spirit hastens to
its God, and the soul nearing its martyrdom longs for
the home which awaits it." Victor then understood that
it was our Lord. He asked him where Paradise was, and
the child said: "Outside this world." "Show it me," said
Victor. "Where then would faith be?" replied the child.
With very natural weakness, Victor said: "I cannot dis-
charge the task you have laid on me. Tell me a sign
which I can invoke." The Lord answered: "Give them the
sign of Jacob."

Brethren, we ought to rejoice at being thus compared
to the patriarchs, if not in righteousness at least in suffering. But he who said: "Call upon me in the time of
trouble, I will save you and you shall glorify me," has
glorified himself; he heard our prayers, he was mindful
of us, promising us the gift of his mercy.

A similar vision was granted to our sister Quartillosa,
who was in prison with us. Her husband and son had both
been martyred three days earlier and she, still with us, was
destined to join her dear ones without delay. She told us
how, in her vision, she saw her son the martyr come into
the prison. He sat down on the edge of the tank, which
was full of water, and said: "God has seen your distress
and sufferings." He was followed by a young man of
wonderful bearing, carrying two bowls of milk, one in
each hand. "Take courage," he said, "God has not forgotten you!" He gave us all to drink from the bowls, and

still they were full. Suddenly the stone which divides the window in two disappeared, and with its removal the windows were flooded with light and gave a free view of the sky. The young man set down his bowls to right and left and said: "Your thirst is quenched, and still there is more. You will see yet a third bowl arrive." So saying, he vanished.

The day after this vision we were waiting the hour for them to bring us our regulation rations, not food, but starvation and misery, for they were no longer giving us anything to eat and we had been fasting for two days. Suddenly, the Lord sent us his support. He arrived like drink given to thirsting men, as food to the famished, as martyrdom to those who long for it. It was our dear Lucian who had brought it. He had got through the prison guards and by the hands of the subdeacon Herennian and Januarius the catechumen—the two bowls in the vision—he gave to us all the Food which never fails. This support was of the greatest encouragement to us in our weakness and trials. Even those who had been made ill by the terrible diet of skilly and cold water recovered their strength, and we all thanked God for his glorious works.

We would now tell you, dear brethren, of our mutual affection, mentioning it only for edification, not to instruct you. As we had been unanimous in the same confession of faith, so we are in our life and our prayer, before the Lord. We must preserve concord and charity and be joined together in the bonds of love; thus do we overthrow the devil and the Lord grants all our requests. We have his express promise in these words: If two of you agree over any request that you make on earth, it will be granted them by my Father who is in heaven.

The only way to gain eternal life and to reign with Christ is to do the will of him who has promised us eternal life and the kingdom of heaven. Only those who have lived in peace with their brethren will receive the inheritance of God. That is the teaching of the Master himself, who has said: Blessed are the peace-makers; they shall be counted the children of God. And St Paul says, expounding these words: We are children of God; and if we are his children, then we are his heirs also; heirs of God, sharing the inheritance of Christ; only we must share his sufferings, if we are to share his glory.

If then we cannot be heirs without being children, and to be children we must be peace-makers, then we cannot share the inheritance of God if we break the peace of God. It was a warning from heaven and a divine vision which recalled this truth to us and now move us to speak of it.

It so happened that some time ago Montanus had been arguing with Julian about an excommunicated woman who had fraudulently gained entrance into our community. Montanus had used reproachful words to Julian and there had been a coolness between them. The following night, Montanus had a vision, which he described thus:

"Some centurions approached and made us march down a long road, till we came to an immense plain, where we were joined by Cyprian and Leucius. At last we reached a place all shining with light; our clothes became white and our bodies even more dazzling than our clothes. Our flesh was transparent, so that our inmost hearts were visible. I looked at my breasts and perceived stains. Still dreaming, I thought I had woken up. I met Lucian, told him what I had seen and said: 'Do you know what caused these stains? It was the fact that I did not at once make up with Julian.' Thereupon I really woke up."

That is why, beloved brethren, we must all at all costs preserve concord, peace and good understanding. We must strive to be in this life what we shall be hereafter. If the promises given to the just concern us, if we fear the punishments which await sinners, if we desire to live and reign with Christ, we must do what leads us to Christ and the kingdom of heaven.

We greet you.

The account of an anonymous chronicler

Thus far is the joint letter of the brethren, which they wrote in prison, but it was necessary to include all the deeds of the blessed martyrs in a complete report. They themselves, in their modesty, did not tell the whole story, and moreover Flavian personally authorized us to supply whatever was omitted from the letter. We have accordingly added what was needed to complete the account.

During their several months' confinement the confessors endured the horrors of the dungeon and suffered long from hunger and thirst. At long last, on the governor's order, they were marched to his praetorium and produced in his court. All bravely confessed their faith.

Flavian had declared that he was a deacon, but his defenders, deluded by affection, maintained that he was no such thing. Sentence of death was passed on the others, Lucius, Montanus, Julian and Victoricus.

Flavian was taken back to prison. He had indeed cause for complaint, seeing himself separated from the company of the others. But the faith and piety which had inspired his life enabled him to see in this trial the will of God. His religion was wise enough to soften his sorrow at being left alone, and he said to himself: "The king's heart is in the hand of God. Why should I be grieved at a man whose decisions are dictated by God?" But about Flavian I shall have more to say later.

Meanwhile the others were escorted to the place of sacrifice, where the pagans flocked in from all sides, and all the brethren were present. Of course they had often before accompanied other witnesses of God, in the religion and faith they had learned in the school of Cyprian, but today they came hither more eagerly and in greater numbers than ever.

Wonderful to behold were these martyrs of Christ, their faces shining with the joy of their glory. Even without words they would have drawn the others after them by their examples. But they spoke untiringly, exhorting their brethren and strengthening their courage. Even Lucius did so. By nature gentle, reserved and modest, he had been weakened to exhaustion by the rigours of the prison. He had gone ahead with some companions, afraid of being swamped by the struggling crowd and so prevented from shedding his blood. He no longer kept silence but did his best to instruct his friends. When some of the brethren said: "Remember us," he replied: "It is for you to remember me." What humility in this martyr, who did not presume on his glory, even at the approach of death!

Julian and Victoricus kept urging the brethren to preserve peace. They commended all the clergy to them, especially those who had been starved in prison. So they arrived at the place of their passion, joyful and unafraid.

Montanus was strong in soul and body. Even before his martyrdom he was well known for his steadfastness and courage in defending the truth, without compromise, but the approach of his martyrdom made him still stronger. With the voice of a prophet he exclaimed: "Whoever sacrifices to the gods and not to the one Lord is doomed to a curse." He repeated these words to all quarters, proclaiming earnestly that it is forbidden to abandon God for the worship of statues, idols made with men's hands. He denounced also the sinful pride and stubbornness of the heretics, adjuring them at least to consider, as they saw this great band of martyrs, where was the true Church, to which they ought to return.

Finally he spoke against the apostates. He condemned

their haste in demanding pardon, saying that their peace with the Church should be deferred till the completion of a full penance, and till the judgement of Christ.

He exhorted those who had held fast to persevere. "Be brave, my brothers, fight valiantly. You have these examples before you; do not let the treason of the apostates lead you into ruin, rather let our constancy raise you to the martyrs' crown." And he called on every virgin to keep pure her holy chastity.

To the company of the faithful he preached respect for authority. To the priests themselves he counselled peace and concord. Nothing was better, he said, than unanimous agreement among the priests, so that the people might be led to respect for the bishops. When the priests are agreed, the people too guards the bonds of charity.

Here was a man ready to suffer for Christ, to imitate Christ in his very words! What a splendid proof of faith! What a fine example of a believer!

The executioner was about to strike, the brandished sword was raised over the martyr's head. The Montanus raised his outstretched hands to the heavens and with a resounding voice, which reached beyond the brethren to the heathen too, he prayed. He asked earnestly that Flavian, who had been separated from the group by the intervention of the public, might follow them on the third day. As a pledge of the efficacy of his prayer, he tore in half the scarf which was to cover his eyes and asked that the other half should be kept to cover Flavian's eyes on the day after the next. He bade us also keep a place for Flavian in the cemetery, among these martyrs, so that he might rest with them even in the grave.

All this came to pass before our eyes, according to our Lord's promise in the Gospel, that he who asks with a firm faith will obtain all he asks. Two days later, in fact, Montanus' prayer was granted, when Flavian followed in his turn and crowned his glorious life with martyrdom. It was Flavian himself, as I said, who told me to complete the narrative, explaining this delay of two days. I would have done so without being asked, but this is another reason for being faithful to his behest.

The crowd, remember, had interfered in his favour: his supporters, moved by misguided friendship, had so frustrated him with their protests for his life that he had been taken back to prison. His courage was undaunted, his spirit unconquerable, his faith unsullied. The thought of being left alone had not weakened his resolution. The prospect might have shaken him, had not his faith been upheld by the hope of a speedy passion so that it trod these passing obstacles underfoot.

Flavian was supported by an incomparable mother. She was of the race of the patriarchs, but proved herself in particular a true daughter of Abraham, being willing even to see her son die. The momentary delay plunged her into a noble distress. What a mother, so religious in her tender affection, worthy to be compared with the examples of old time, a noble emulator of the mother of the Machabees! What matters the number of her sons, since she too had sacrificed all her affections by offering to the Lord her only son?

Flavian praised his mother's sentiments, but would not have her distressed at his being remanded. "You know, darling mother," he said, "how much I desired, if I should have the joy of confessing my faith in God, to taste my martyrdom to the full, to bear my chains long in public, to be often remanded. If he now grants my prayer, we should not weep but rejoice."

On the day of his death there was more difficulty than usual in opening the gate of the prison and it took more time, despite the efforts of the gaolers. Some spirit seemed to be holding it shut, as if it were protesting against this disgraceful treatment, which condemned to the horrors of a dungeon a man whose home was already prepared in heaven. But God had good reasons for postponing the martyr's crown. At last the prison opened to allow passage to the man of heaven, the man of God.

Flavian's feelings during these two days, his hope and confidence, can be imagined: he trusted in his companions' prayer and, for his part, believed that his passion was near. To my mind, after these two days in prison he was awaiting the third as the day, not of his passion, but of his resurrection. Astonishment spread even to the pagans, who had heard Montanus' prayer.

On the third day, Flavian was ordered to be produced. At this news, unbelievers and heretics ran together, to see the martyr's faith put to the proof. God's witness left the prison, never to return. Great was the joy of all the brethren, but happiest of all was the martyr. He was sure that the faith and prayer of his companions, martyred before him, would force the governor, in spite of himself and in spite of the protests of the crowd, to pronounce sentence of death, and when the brethren ran forward to greet him he promised them, in complete confidence, to give them the kiss of peace at Fuscianum, the place of execution. What gallant confidence, what true faith!

He came into the praetorium and standing there, waiting to be called, he was the admiration of all in the guard-room. I was close beside him, touching him, and kept my hands in his, to show him my respect for the martyr, my affection for my friend.

His pupils begged him with tears to give in, if only for a moment, and sacrifice, and then do what he liked after-wards. Why should he be more afraid of a later, uncertain death, than of this which was imminent? These were heathen thoughts. For them it seemed the height of folly to fear the pains of an imagined eternal death, and to lose this present life. Flavian thanked them for their signs of friendship, for they were trying to save him, to their way of thinking. He spoke to them about faith and God. "Better far to keep one's conscience free and accept death than to worship stones. There is a supreme God who has made all things; he alone should be worshipped." He added something which the pagans can scarcely admit, even when they believe in God: "We live on still, even when we are killed. We are death's victors, not its victims. You too, if you wish to find the truth, ought to become Christians."

Rebuffed and confounded by his words, his defenders, finding their advice of no avail, pressed their sympathy to the point of cruelty. They imagined that the confessor's resolution would yield at least to torture.

When Flavian was brought in, the governor asked him why he had lied by calling himself a deacon, when he was not. Flavian said that he was. Then a centurion claimed to have received a letter proving that the accused was dissembling. Flavian replied, "Why think me the liar, and not the author of this fraud?" The crowd protested with cries of "You lie!" and again the governor asked if indeed he lied. "What good would it do me to lie?" he replied.

At these words the crowd in exasperation shouted for the accused to be put to the torture. But the Lord, who already knew his martyr's faith through the trials of the prison, would not allow any instrument of torture to wound, even a little, the body of the martyr who had already proved his courage. He touched the heart of the magistrate, who at once pronounced sentence of death. The martyr had run his course, he was proving victorious in the fight, and the Lord wished to crown his witness, faithful unto death.

Now Flavian was completely happy. The sentence made

him certain of martyrdom, and he was now cheerful in his speech. It was then that he charged me to write this story and to add it to his own account. He specially wished the visions to be added, for part of them referred to these two days of reprieve. Then he said:

"When our bishop Cyprian was still the only one to have died a martyr, this is what I saw. I seemed to be talking with Cyprian and asking him if the blow hurt, in the shock of death. Destined to martyrdom in my turn, I wanted to learn what endurance was necessary. The bishop replied: 'It is another's flesh which suffers when the soul is in heaven. The body feels nothing more, when our thought is wholly hidden in God.' "

Magnificent words of one martyr to another! The one declares that the death-blow is painless, to encourage the other who is to be stricken in his turn. Thenceforth the martyr knows that he has not to fear the least sensation of pain under the fatal stroke.

Flavian continued: "Later on, when my companions were nearly all martyred, I dreamed at night and gave myself up to sadness, at the thought of remaining alone, far from my friends. Then a man appeared and said; 'Why are you sad?' I told him the reason, and he replied: 'And are you sad? Twice you have confessed the faith, and the third time you will be martyred with the sword.' "

So, indeed, it fell out. After a first confession of faith in the audience-chamber Flavian confessed Christ a second time, in public. It was then that the crowd had protested. Taken back to prison, he was parted from his companions, as he had been warned in his vision. After these two confessions he was handed over, a third time, and it was then that he achieved martyrdom.

Flavian then told us: "Successus and Paul had just received the crown of martyrdom with their companions, and I myself had scarcely recovered from illness, when

I saw the bishop Successus coming into my house. His face and clothes glistened with light; it was hard to recognize him, his eyes shone with such angelic brilliance. Seeing my hesitation, he said: "I am sent to announce your approaching martyrdom." At these words, two soldiers appeared to lead me out. They took me to a place where a great crowd of our brethren was assembled. I appeared before the governor and was condemned to death. Suddenly I saw my mother in the middle of the crowd, and she called out: 'Well done! Never was known such a glorious martyr!' "

It was a true word. Need I speak of the starvation-diet imposed in the prison? The other prisoners still accepted the miserable pittance doled out by the authorities in their sordid avarice, but Flavian alone would not touch his minute portion. He left it to the others, to keep them alive, preferring for himself to be exhausted in complete and voluntary fasts.

Now I come to the greatest matter for boasting. Flavian was alone in his march to the place of death, but never was anyone conducted with such honours. The priests whom he had trained formed his escort, seeming to follow him as their leader. This triumphal march showed clearly that the martyr, so soon to share in the divine kingship, already reigned here below in heart and spirit.

The heavens themselves bore witness to it, for a kindly rain began to fall, in warm, heavy showers. It came opportunely, checking the curiosity of the pagans and allowing the faithful to gather round him in a circle, so that no non-Christian could take part in the last kiss of peace. In the event, as Flavian himself remarked, this rain fell just in time to mingle water with the blood, as in our Lord's passion.

When he had bidden farewell to all the brethren and given them all the kiss of peace, Flavian left the shed where he had taken shelter, close to Fuscianum. Standing up on a mound, to be heard the better, he made a gesture for silence and said:

"Beloved brethren, you will rest in peace with us if you remain in peace with the Church and preserve unity in charity. And this is no light thing to say, for our Lord Jesus Christ himself, on the eve of his Passion, left us these words: My commandment is that you love one another, as I have loved you."

Flavian ended his discourse with this supreme exhortation, which he sealed, like a legacy, with the last words of his faith. He highly praised the priest Lucian, thereby naming him as the next bishop of Carthage; a well-deserved choice. Insight is naturally very clear, when heaven and Christ are so close at hand.

His speech ended, he came down from the mound and went to the place of execution. There he bound his eyes with the scarf which Montanus had asked to be kept, two days before, for this purpose. Then he knelt down to pray, and still praying he consummated his martyrdom.

Marinus (at Caesarea, A.D. 262)

In the time when there was peace everywhere in all the Churches, Marinus, an officer in the army, a man eminent by birth and wealth, was beheaded at Caesarea in Palestine on account of his witness for Christ. The occasion was as follows:

There is an honour among the Romans known as the "vine-switch," and they who obtain it are called centurions. There being a place vacant, his rank in the service entitled Marinus to this promotion. When he was on the point of succeeding to this honour some one appeared before the tribunal, and alleged that it was not lawful for him according to ancient precedent to have any part in the dignities of Rome, since he was a Christian, and did not sacrifice to the Emperors; and that the position fell to himself.

The judge, moved thereat (his name was Achaeus), first asked Marinus what his opinions were, and when he saw that he resolutely confessed himself a Christian, gave him three hours interval for consideration.

When he came outside the court, Theotecnus, the bishop of that district, went up to him in friendly fashion, talked at length with him, and taking him by the hand led the way to the church, entered and placed him close to the very altar. He then drew back Marinus' cloak a little, and pointed to the sword as it hung at his side; at the same time he brought him the book of the Gospels, bidding him choose that which was to his mind. When he at once stretched out his right hand and took the Divine Scriptures, "Hold fast, then," said Theotecnus to him, "Hold fast to God, and may you, strengthened by him, obtain what you have chosen. Go in peace."

And immediately on his return from there the voice of the crier was heard in front of the court calling for him; for already the time allowed him was fulfilled. So he stood before the judge, and after showing zeal beyond belief, was forthwith, as he was, led forth to death and died a martyr.

CHAPTER V

FROM DIOCLETIAN'S PERSECUTIONS TO FINAL VICTORY

The supreme effort of the Roman power against Christianity was Diocletian's persecution. Since his accession in 283 this emperor had restored the strength of the empire, which he had found gravely impaired, by adopting a colleague, Maximian, to help him in a task which was growing ever more onerous. Though deeply imbued with the old Roman spirit, for the space of some twenty years he had shown no sign of any hostility to Christianity, which continued to make many converts. There were some, as we know, among the high officials of the imperial court.

But all this changed at the beginning of the fourth century. Diocletian had not taken long to decide that a single collaborator with the emperor was no longer enough for the protection of the empire. To his colleague Maximian and himself, the two Augusti, he had assigned two associates, called the Caesars, destined in due course to be their successors. It happened that one of the two Caesars, Galerius, chosen for his military valour as the direct associate of Diocletian, was a determined enemy of the Christians, against whom, as well, certain intellectual circles were on the defensive and always ready to

attack them. Galerius was thus able to win over Diocletian, now growing old and less strong-minded with age,
to his views. Persecution once more broke out, not immediately in all its brutality, but in a series of progressive
measures which, in rapid stages, once again presented
the whole body of Christian believers with the tragic alter-
native of apostasy or death.

There were three successive edicts in 303. The first
ordered the destruction of the churches and the sacred
books, dismissed Christians from all offices, dignities or
privileges they could hold, deprived them of the right to
plead at law and forbade Christian slaves ever to be
emancipated. The next ordered the imprisonment of the
clergy, and the third, torture for all who refused to sacrifice. A fourth in the next year, reviving the desperate
attempt of Decius fifty years before, extended the obligation to sacrifice to all the faithful.

The massacre began, though very unequally in different
places. The application of the edicts was in fact most
lenient in Gaul and Britain, which were under the authority of the Caesar Constantius Chlorus, father of the
future emperor Constantine, and certainly a favourer
of Christianity. It was the same, from the following year,
in Spain, when the abdication of Diocletian brought this
country under the rule of Chlorus, who had become
Augustus and chief of the imperial college. But the victims
were numerous in Italy, where many Christians perished
whose heroism has become renowned: Pope Marcellinus,
Mark, Peter and Agnes in Rome, Lucy at Syracuse, at
Imola the schoolmaster Cassian, who perished at the hands
of his pupils; in Rhaetia we have the names of Afra, a
converted courtesan, at Augusta (Augsburg), in Africa
those of Innocent at Milevis, of Nivalis, Matrona and
Salvus at Calama (Guelma), Digna at Rusicada (Philip-
peville), the matron Crispina at Theveste (Tebessa),

Justus and Secundus at Sitifis (Sétif), Fabius, standard-bearer to the governor of Mauretania; Maxima Secunda at Thuburbo, and forty-eight Christians of Abitene, under Saturninus their priest. There were the unknown martyrs revealed by an inscription at Ammoedara in proconsular Africa, which does not give their names; in Spain the deacon Vincent at Valentia, Felix at Girona, Cucufas at Barcelona, Aciselus and Zoellus at Cordova, and the young Eulalia at Merida. All these give only a very inadequate idea of the number of martyrs from the provinces governed by Diocletian's immediate colleague, in the last persecution. Peace was restored here in 305. But in the Illyrian provinces, in Asia Minor, in Syria and the rest of the East, as in Egypt, the fanaticism of Galerius and his nephew and successor Maximin Daia was for long unchecked, and men and women of every class honoured the Danubian Churches by their deaths: bishops like St Philip of Heraclea, Irenaeus of Sirmium, Domnius of Salom, Quirinus of Siscia, Victorinus of Paetovio (Pettau), priests such as Severus and Montanus, deacons such as Demetrius and Septimius, minor clergy, conse-crated virgins, layfolk of both sexes and many others whose names are recorded, though nothing else is known of them but their faith and their valour, besides countless others, no doubt, whose very names are forgotten. In Cilicia, Cappadocia and Galatia there were whole heca-tombs of clergy and laity. Syria and Palestine, to whose martyrs Eusebius of Caesarea, the Church's first historian, devoted a special book, paid a particularly heavy tribute. It was in Egypt, that "China of the ancient world," that the persecution seems to have reached its highest degree of cruelty. Neither men, women nor children were spared, and the executioners used their utmost ingenuity to devise new tortures. So much so, indeed, that sometimes the pagans were overcome by pity, as had happened before, and began to help the Christians to escape the fate which awaited them. Thus public opinion, so long hostile or at least suspicious, and then perplexed, now began to change and was at last compelled to confess the existence of those virtues which it did not always understand, and this gradually led to sympathy.

It was perhaps because they were dimly conscious of this that after the abdication of Diocletian and Maximian some of the new emperors, led by Constantius Chlorus, without abrogating the persecuting edicts, allowed the persecution to drop. But in the East it continued and in some regions became even more severe, up to a sudden change of mind on the part of Galerius. Afflicted with a frightful disease, from which he was practically crumbling alive into dust, and in which he had every reason to see a divine punishment, he decided in April 311 to publish an edict which was really a charter of liberty for the Church. It proclaimed, though with a bad grace, the right of the Christians to profess and practice their religion, individually and corporately by holding meetings for worship and, correlatively, the restoration of ecclesiastical property. The age of the persecutions was followed by the peace of the Church, as it has been called. Constantine, son of Constantius Chlorus, who in his turn became emperor in 311 and was already half a Christian while intending to become one fully, after all only confirmed and ensured the peace by his imperial declarations in 312, known, though inaccurately, as the Edict of Milan.

The age of the persecutions was over. However great the number of victims may have been, it is doubtful whether it can be compared with that in the massacres which later afflicted the Christians of the Middle Ages in the Arab conquests, or in the Mongol invasions, though these were not aimed at Christians in particular, any more than the cold and implacable Communist liquidations in our days. Nonetheless the Church had paid dearly for the recognition of her right to exist in the Roman empire and to obey her Master's bidding to preach to all nations.

When we consider that this peaceful conquest had been achieved in only two hundred and fifty years, its extent was enormous. The Christians, it is true, were only a minority at this time, in some regions in the West still a very small one, though much bigger and even a majority in certain provinces or districts in the East. It was still mainly the towns which had been won, the countryside being as yet scarcely touched. Christianity was still principally, in geographical fact, a religion of the cities.

In the main, too, it was still a religion of the poor and humble. In the middle of the third century Origen makes no difficulty about admitting that it is drawn chiefly from "weavers, fullers and shoemakers." But it had begun to spread considerably among all classes of society. Tertullian, earlier than Origen, speaks of the Christian *clarissimi,* that is, members of the Roman senatorial aristocracy, and the provincial middle class provided a growing number of converts to the Christian religion, as appears from the conversion of an increasing number of men like the bishops Gregory of Neocaesarea in Pontus or Cyprian of Carthage, advocates or relations of magistrates, or of women like the "matron" Perpetua in Africa, and so many others, members of the curias or municipal councils, from Asia Minor to Spain, while many were found in the emperor's court.

The facts thus give the lie to the too often accepted idea that the Christians were not good citizens. Their true fatherland is indeed beyond this world, but apart from some statements of extremist writers like Tertullian, whose ideas are tinged with rhetoric, apart from some exalted utterances of Christians in the dock, we have no grounds for considering the early Christians as defective citizens, citizens of second grade, as they say nowadays. If there were conscientious objectors, as there certainly were, the Church never formally ratified their attitude and more than once reproved it. But it is very certain that the Christian mentality could never coincide at all points with that of the ancient state, and it was precisely a difference of spirit which made Christians appear unreliable citizens in the eyes of authority and Roman opinion, both of cultivated society and of the common people. Respectful to the laws, obedient to the emperor, loyal to the empire, they still did not set their country "above all else." Looking as they did beyond the frontiers and beyond time, they could naturally be reproached with a certain indifference to the safety of the empire and *a fortiori* to its extension. But their private virtues, contempt for wealth, purity in morals and their boundless charity made them in fact the very pick of the citizens. Towards the world beyond the frontiers they had, too, an attitude, even if only implicit, noticeably different from that of their fellow-citizens, who were always rather lacking in curiosity about what went on outside. This interest in the outside world was something which the Christians, on the contrary, were bound to have at heart, since they desired to evangelize it, and this concern certainly did not run counter to the well understood interests of Roman civilization. Obviously, in looking beyond the bounds of that civilization, the Christians were obedient to a higher mission than its extension. But it is historically very important to note that while about the year 300 the empire was still within its traditional boundaries (which a great victory of Diocletian at the beginning of his reign had just carried to the Tigris), the visible kingdom of Christ already overflowed them in all directions. It had already begun to pass them, both in Britain and in North Africa, but more particularly beyond the Danube and the Caucasus, the Tigris and the Nile, having reached Abyssinia, penetrated Persia and affected at least the approaches of India.

So vast an extent, gained in comparatively so short a time and in spite of so many adverse factors, engenders the thought that this movement was guided by a providential purpose. It is true that its way had been prepared by a religious development which had grown up alongside the Christian, but this was as much an obstacle as an advantage. The success in the Roman world of oriental religions like those of Phrygia, Egypt and above all Persia, proves that men's minds were generally attracted to monotheism; but the followers of those religions were often among the bitterest enemies of Christianity, which they regarded as their great rival, and since they had lower moral standards and moreover allowed their members to take part in the traditional cults of Rome and its emperor-worship, for that reason they often enjoyed the favour of its rulers, their final triumph might naturally have been foretold. But it was not so and, in spite of holding all the trumps, humanly speaking, the various eastern religions, and finally solar monotheism which, as it were, summed them all up, failed to achieve a lasting hold on men's minds, so much so that when, after Constantine's conversion, they lacked state protection, their decline was so marked that in a little more than a century they were only a memory.

If the apparent paradox of the Christian triumph is that it was obtained in so relatively short a time, despite the triple opposition of the power of the State, the popular masses and "enlightened" opinion, it is found also in the attitude adopted by the Christians in face of this hostility: they opposed it with only passive resistance, in strict conformity with the spirit and the letter of the Gospel on submitting to blows; for two hundred and fifty years they accepted martyrdom with a calm heroism which ended by producing conversions.

For all that, they did not simply reconcile themselves to the evil which persecution is in itself, but constantly opposed it with purely spiritual weapons, prayer and the effort to persuade, such as that of the apologists, which for long had little visible effect. But Christianity steadily increased its membership, till in the end the hostile power wearied of persecuting, while the enmity of the masses was gradually softened by the beauty of Christians' lives and the heroism of Christians' deaths.

No one would be prepared to deny out of hand that such a result, in face of adverse factors, could appear so improbable that it seems practically inconceivable unless it had been prepared and upheld by a plan of Providence. But it was through human factors that this preparation was brought about, and any light thrown on the historical factors which explain the victory of Christianity will only make clearer the unique character of the power that informed it.

To consider first only the external aspect of affairs, it is certain that the unification of a great part of the known world by the Roman empire provided undeniable facilities for the spread of the Gospel message. That so many countries formerly distinct and often mutually hostile now formed one vast network of lands where peace reigned could obviously only favour the progress of the message and the establishment of the organization which went with it. But above all, this message responded to a human aspiration which, consciously or unconsciously, but increasingly as time went on, had long awaited an answer, but never yet received it. It was an aspiration to a fullness of being which life denies to the majority of men, and even if it were granted it would be inexorably precarious, being cut short by death. It is then an aspiration to immortality, an immortality of happiness, and of a higher sort than that offered by earthly life, that is what Christianity came to satisfy, with its promise of union with God in an endless love, through the redemption wrought by Jesus Christ. Such a message was offered, admittedly, by other religions which like it came from the East, but under very different conditions from those of Christianity. The fulfilment of their promises of life was conditional on the knowledge of mysteries supposed to be renewed by the practice of rites which were purely formal, and even if they were connected with a preparatory purification, this was far more external than internal, more bodily than spiritual. However essential Christianity has always declared its own mysteries to be, as proceeding directly or indirectly from the commands of its Founder, it has always taught that they are intimately bound up with the notion of charity, that is, with the fatherly love of God for men, the filial love of men for God and the brotherly love of men for one another, along with the requirement of a moral virtue which is simply the practical application of this charity in all fields. None of the eastern religions which tried to challenge Christianity for the conquest of men's souls not even the highest, like Mithraism, had spoken in accents to be compared with those of St Paul in his praise of charity, which supplies for everything and without which all the rest is nothing.

Many men felt that here was something new, and it impressed them. This was what explained that superhuman courage and serenity in the face of death which was disconcerting, sometimes irritating, but which gradually compelled admiration and won their sympathies, not only for men who could give such examples, but also for the doctrines they professed. This apologetic of martyrdom, expressed in Tertullian's saying: "The blood of the martyrs is the seed of the Church," joined hands with the apologetic of charity. When, on the morrow of a persecution, as during the plague which followed the Decian persecution, the survivors were seen to be spending themselves in the service of a whole town ravaged by the epidemic, or of another, half destroyed by an earthquake, how could the beholders fail to be moved, to reflect and to question themselves at sight of such a lesson?

Add to this that there had long been an élite in pagan society, in Rome and elsewhere, who were not satisfied with the fables of paganism and the moral poverty of the old Greco-Roman polytheism, but were also repelled by the inhuman stiffness of Stoicism, and we can understand what the attraction of Christianity must have been. Thus Christianity spoke to the heart as well as to the mind, as no other doctrine had spoken to them before.

It spoke, moreover, to the hearts and minds of all men. The universalist character of the Christian religion is the supreme factor in its conquering power, a factor both social and moral. The appeal of Christianity was to all, great and small, rich and poor, educated and simple, and all found their happiness by responding to it.

No doubt there were other ancient religions which had not raised a bar against anyone, but they were religions of the State, and those who counted for little in the State counted for little more in them. Some of the eastern religions were more welcoming and took no account of social rank, but in accepting a sort of fusion with the State religions they became State religions too, and the common folk could then hardly feel at home in them. In contrast, Christianity came forward from the outset as a religion of the poor. To the sarcasms of its adversaries, like Celsus, on this point, the declarations of Tertullian and Origen replied significantly enough, and yet during the first three centuries of its history it never ceased to attract increasingly the social, intellectual and moral élite of this world. It was indeed the religion for all men. That is why from all sides, in spite of every kind of opposition, they flocked to it.

CONTEMPORARY DOCUMENTS

CHRISTIAN LIFE AND PRAYER

(From the compilation called *The Apostolic Constitutions*, A.D. 380.)

Litany

We beseech thee, O Lord, for thy holy Church from one end of the world to the other, which thou hast acquired by the precious blood of thy Christ: keep it unshaken, sheltered from storms, till the end of the ages.

We beseech thee for the universal episcopate, which faithfully hands on the word of truth.

We beseech thee for the lowliness of thy celebrant, and for all the presbyterate, for the deacons and the clergy, that all may be filled with the wisdom of thy Spirit.

We beseech thee for the king and those in authority, for all the army, that we may dwell in peace, so that we may spend our lives in tranquillity and concord, to glorify thee through Jesus Christ, our hope.

We offer unto thee for all the saints who from the beginning have pleased thee, for the patriarchs, prophets, just men, martyrs, confessors, bishops, priests, deacons, subdeacons, readers, cantors, virgins, widows, laity and all whose names are known to thee.

We offer unto thee for this people, that it may become the praise of Christ, a royal priesthood, a holy nation; for those who live in virginity and chastity, for the Church's widows, for those who live in chaste wedlock and bear children unto thee, for the babes of thy people, that thou mayest reject no one among us.

We beseech thee for this city and all its inhabitants, for the sick, for the poor slaves, for the exiles, for those in prison, the travellers by sea or land; uphold them all, be to all a refuge and defence.

We beseech thee for all who hate us and persecute us for thy Name's sake, for those who are without and are wandering, that thou mayest lead them back to goodness and soften their wrath.

We beseech thee for the Church's catechumens, for those who are tempted by the Adversary and for our brethren who are doing penance; strengthen the first in the faith; deliver the second from the assaults of the evil one; accept the penitence of the last and pardon their offences, and ours.

We offer unto thee for fair weather and abundant harvests, that we who are ever receiving benefits from thy hand may praise thee without ceasing, thou who givest food to all flesh.

Finally we praise thee on behalf of those who are lawfully absent, that thou mayest keep us all in godliness and gather us all into the kingdom of thy Christ, the God of all things visible and intelligent, and our King; keep us steadfast, blameless and without reproach.

Through him is due to thee glory, worship, thanksgiving, honour and adoration, with the Father and the Holy Spirit, now and ever, to infinite and eternal ages!
And all the people answer:
Amen.

Before the communion
The bishop says to the people:
Holy things for the holy!
The people answers:
One only is holy, one only is the Lord, one Jesus

Christ, to the glory of God the Father, blessed for ever. Amen.

Glory to God in the highest heavens, peace on earth, goodwill to men. Hosanna to the Son of David!

Blessed is he who comes in the name of the Lord. The Lord is God, he has appeared to us. Hosanna in the highest heavens!

Prayer of thanksgiving

O Lord, God, the almighty, Father of thy Christ, the blessed Son, who hearest the prayer which is uttered in righteousness and knowest also the silent desires of our hearts, we thank thee for that thou has counted us worthy to partake of thy holy mysteries, which thou hast given us for the fullness of the faith, to preserve us in goodness and to forgive us our sins, for the name of thy Christ is invoked upon us and we belong to thy household.

As thou hast separated us from the company of the wicked and united us to those who are consecrated to thee, establish us in the truth by the coming of the Holy Spirit, reveal to us the things that are unknown, fill up what we lack and confirm what we have learned.

Preserve thy priests blameless in thy service, maintain kings in peace and governors in justice, grant us fair weather and abundant harvests and keep the world in thy all-sufficient providence; curb warlike nations, bring back to the right path those who have strayed. Sanctify thy people, protect the virgins, keep the married in faithfulness, strengthen the reconciled, bring the children to maturity, strengthen the new converts, teach the catechumens and make them worthy to be initiated, and bring us all together at last to the kingdom of the heavens in Christ Jesus our Saviour.

To him, and to thee and the Holy Spirit, be glory, honour and worship for ever! Amen.

The bishop's final blessing

Almighty God, true and incomparable, present every-where, present to all and dependent on none, who art not confined to one place, who growest not old with the ages; undeceived by words, without beginning, needing no protection, above all corruption, not subject to change, immutable in nature, dwelling in light inaccessible; invisible in essence, making thyself known to all rational beings who seek thee diligently, God of the Israel which beholds, of the people which believes in Christ.

Mercifully hear me for thy name's sake and bless those who have bowed their heads; grant them the desires of their hearts which are good for them and shut not one of them out of thy kingdom. Sanctify them, guard them, protect them, uphold them, deliver them from the Enemy and from every foe, watch over their dwellings and keep their coming in and their going out.

For to thee are due the glory, the praise, the exaltation, the worship and adoration, with thy Son, Jesus, thy Christ, our Lord, our God and our King, and with the Holy Spirit, now and always and for endless ages! Amen.
And the deacon says:
Go in peace.

PRAYERS FOR VARIOUS OCCASIONS

(Book VII of the *Apostolic Constitutions* provides various forms of prayer. The first thirty-three chapters are influenced by the *Didache,* the others seem to depend on an ancient ritual.)

Prayer in praise of God's providence

Eternal Saviour and King of all hosts, thou only art almighty and Lord, God of all creation, God of our holy and blameless Fathers who were before us, God of

Abraham, of Isaac and of Jacob, full of pity and compassion, of pity and mercy. Every heart is open to thee and our most secret thoughts are not hidden from thee. Father of the just, thou hearest those who pray to thee in sincerity, thou hearest even our silent pleas; thy providence searches man's reins and thy knowledge reveals the will of every man. From every region of the earth the incense of prayer and supplication ascends to thee.

Thou hast made our mortal life an arena, in which all run to attain justice; to all thou openest the gates of thy mercy. Thou hast shown to all men, by their inborn knowledge and natural judgement and by the light of thy Law, that riches are not eternal, that beauty is transitory, the strongest powers are dissolved; that all is smoke and vanity: nothing abides but the consciousness of a pure faith, nothing else travels the road to heaven with truth and finds heavenly joys within its reach. Until the promise of the new birth is fulfilled by the resurrection, the soul overflows with joy in hope.

In the beginning thou didst guide Abraham our father in the way of truth, showing him thyself; thou didst teach him the meaning of this present world. Knowledge preceded his faith, faith followed knowledge, the covenant followed the faith. For thou didst say: I will multiply thy posterity as the stars of the sky, and as the sand upon the sea-shore. Even so when he gave him Isaac, whom he knew must resemble his father—he would be called the God of Isaac—he said to him: I shall be thy God and the God of thy posterity after thee. When our father Jacob set out for Mesopotamia thou didst say (showing forth Christ in him): I am with thee, I shall increase and multiply thy posterity. And to Moses, thy holy and faithful servant, thou didst say, in the vision of the bush: I am who am. This is my name for ever, and this is my memorial unto all generations.

Defender of the race of Abraham, thou art blessed for ever.

Prayer in praise of creation

Blessed art thou, O Lord, King of the ages. Through Christ thou hast created the universe, thou hast given order to the formless world; thou hast separated the waters beneath from the waters above the firmament, thou hast breathed into them the breath of life, thou hast established the earth and stretched out the heavens; to every creature thou hast given its appointed place.

Through thy power, O sovereign Lord, the world was established in splendour, the heaven as a vault, lit up with stars, to comfort us in the night; the sun and its light appeared to shine in the day and ripen the harvests, the waxing and waning moon to measure the seasons. They were named the day and the night, and the firmament arose from among the deeps. Thou badest the waters to be gathered together, that the dry land might appear.

The sea's praises who can sing? It is let loose and comes in from the ocean, and thither returns when thou dost forbid it to pass the shore. For thou hast said: its waves shall be broken. There hast thou traced a way for the fishes, great and small, and for the sailors.

And the earth brought forth, in the tapestry of its flowers and the variety of its trees, and the shining stars which give them light follow their unvarying course, never transgressing thy commands. According to thy decrees they rise and set, to mark the seasons and the years, regulating man's labour.

Next appeared the various kinds of animals, on land and in the water, and the amphibians; the ordered wisdom of thy providence gives to each according to its need:

the same power which presided over their creation still watches over the needs of all.

To complete creation according to the orders of thy wisdom, thou madest the creature which is endowed with reason, to inhabit the earth, saying: Let us make man in our image and our likeness. And thou madest him the world of the world, the splendour of splendours. Thou madest his body of the four elements already existing, but his soul thou didst draw from nothing, thou gavest its five senses and the spirit which rules them.

Furthermore, O sovereign Lord, who can worthily tell of the movement of the rain-bearing clouds, of the lightning-flash, the crash of thunder? All things are so ordered as to give every man according to his need, with the greatest variety of temperature.

When man sinned, thou didst withdraw the life promised him in reward, yet thou didst not utterly destroy it, but keepest it veiled for a season. By an oath thou didst call him to the new birth. Thou didst tear up the decree of death, thou who restorest life to the dead, through Jesus Christ, our hope.

Thanksgiving on Sunday

Lord almighty, thou didst create the world through Christ, and in memory of this creation didst institute the sabbath, so that man, being freed from his work, might meditate on thy Law. Thou didst appoint festival days, to rejoice our souls, to recall thy wisdom which comes from thee.

For our sakes, the uncreated Wisdom willed to be born of a woman. He appeared in our mortal life, and at his baptism he showed that he was God and man; with thy consent he suffered for us; he died and rose again in power.

Therefore, celebrating thy resurrection on the Lord's Day, we rejoice that he has overcome death and brought us the light of life and immortality.

Through him thou hast led the nations to thyself, to form the chosen people, the true Israel, the beloved people which sees God.

Of old, O Lord, thou didst bring our fathers out from the land of Egypt, thou didst snatch them from the furnace of fire, from the making of pots and bricks. Thou didst save them from the hand of Pharao and his minions; thou madest them to pass through the sea as on dry land, and in the desert bestowedst on them many good things.

Thou gavest them the Law, the Ten Commandments, pronounced by thy mouth and written with thy hand. Thou didst institute the sabbath, not for an occasion of idleness but to encourage piety; to prevent them, as held in a sacred septenary, from doing evil, to instruct them and give them the joy of the week. That is the express purpose of the week, of the seven weeks, of the seventh month, of the seventh year and its periodical return, of the jubilee, the fiftieth year, the year of pardon. So that men might have no excuse for their ignorance, God instituted the sabbath rest, so that on this day they should utter not even a word of anger.

The sabbath is the rest after creation, the consummation of the world, the seeking of the Law, the thanksgiving to God for the gifts he has given to man. But the Lord's Day excels all others. It speaks to us of the Mediator, the Provider, the Lawgiver, the author of the Resurrection, the firstborn of all creation, the Word, God and man, born of Mary without human aid, who lived in justice, was crucified under Pontius Pilate, died and rose again from the dead.

For all these gifts, sovereign Lord, the Lord's Day

exhorts us to offer thee praise, for grace has been given us to declare in their greatness all thy benefits.

Prayer of the young converts

God Almighty, Father of Christ, thy only Son, grant me a body without stain, a pure heart, a watchful spirit, knowledge without error, the coming of the Spirit, that I may possess and establish the truth, through thy Christ, through whom, in the Holy Spirit, be glory to thee for evermore! Amen.

The evening prayer

Praise the Lord, ye children, praise the name of the Lord. We praise thee, we hymn thee, we bless thee, because of thy great glory.

O Lord, King, Father of Christ, of the spotless Lamb, who bears the sin of the world; to thee be praise, to thee be hymns, to thee be glory, to the Father and the Son and the Holy Spirit, for ever and ever! Amen.

Nunc dimittis . . .

BISHOP SARAPION'S PRAYER-BOOK

(Until the end of the last century, we possess no liturgical document from Christian Egypt comparable to the *Apostolic Constitutions* from Syria. That lack has been made good by the discovery at Mount Athos of a euchology or prayer-book, containing thirty prayers, two of which bear the name of Sarapion of Thmuis, the friend of St Athanasius. The others are most probably by the same author (about 350).

The prayers of this collection belong to the Sunday office and the eucharistic liturgy, baptism, ordination, the blessing of oils, and funerals.)

The eucharistic liturgy: first prayer
of the Lord's Day

We beseech thee, Father of the only-begotten Son, Lord of the whole world, Creator of all creatures, Author of all that exists; we raise pure hands to thee and unfold our hearts to thee, O Lord.

. . . Look upon us, O Lord; we display to thee our weaknesses. Grant thy pardon and pity to all of us here in common; pity thy people, grant it to be gentle, sober and pure; send angelic powers, that thy whole people may be acknowledged holy and immaculate.

I pray thee to send holy Spirit into our souls and grant us to learn the Scriptures from thy inspiration, and to interpret them purely and worthily, that all the people here present may be profited, through thy only-begotten Son in holy Spirit, through whom to thee is the glory and the power, now and for ever. Amen.

Prayer after the Sermon

O God, Saviour, God of the universe, Lord and Creator of all that exists, begetter of the only-begotten, who has begotten thy living and true Image, who didst send him to help the race of men, and through him didst call men and take possession of them; we beseech thee for this assembled people; send them holy Spirit and let the Lord Jesus visit them, let him speak in the minds of all and dispose their hearts to faith; may he draw their souls to thee, O God of mercies.

Take possession too of a people in this city, create a chosen flock, through thy only-begotten Jesus Christ in holy Spirit, through whom to thee is the glory and the power, now and for ever. Amen.

Prayer over the Catechumens

Saviour and Lord of all, Liberator of the liberated, Protector of the redeemed, Hope of those who have come under thy mighty hand: thou hast done away sin, through thy Only-begotten thou hast destroyed the works of Satan and loosed his devices and delivered those who were bound by him.

We thank thee on behalf of the Catechumens, for thou hast been pleased to call them through thy Only-begotten and to bestow on them thy knowledge. Wherefore confirm them, we pray, in this knowledge, that they may know thee, the one true God, and him whom thou hast sent, Jesus Christ, that they may be kept pure, through thy teachings, and may advance. Make them worthy of the washing of the new birth and of the holy mysteries, through the only-begotten Jesus Christ in holy Spirit, through whom to thee is the glory and the power, now and for ever. Amen.

Blessing of the Catechumens

To thee, O Lord, we stretch forth our hands and pray thee to stretch forth thy divine and living hands to bless this people. To thee, Father uncreated, through the Only-begotten, they have bowed their heads.

May thy blessing be upon this people for the grace of knowledge and piety, for the grace which flows from thy mysteries, through thy only-begotten Jesus Christ, through whom to thee is the glory and the power, now and for ever. Amen.

Prayer over the people

We confess to thee, O God who lovest men, and we bring before thee our weakness, praying thee to be our strength. Pardon our past sins, remit our faults of former times and make us new men. Make us thy servants, pure and blameless; we dedicate ourselves to thee; receive us, O God of truth, receive thy people and make us wholly without reproach; cause us to live in innocence and purity; let us be worthy to be counted among the angels, that all may be elect and holy.

We pray thee for those who have come to believe and have come to know the Lord Jesus Christ, that they may be confirmed in the faith and the knowledge and the doctrine.

We pray thee for this people: be merciful to all, make thyself known, reveal thy light, that all may know thee as the uncreated Father, and thy only-begotten Son Jesus Christ.

We pray for all rulers, that their government may be peaceful, for the peace of the Catholic Church.

We pray thee, O God of mercies, for free men and slaves, for men and women, old and young, poor and rich; show to all thy kindness, to all extend thy goodness, have pity on all and guide their steps to thee.

We pray thee for the travellers; send them the angel of peace to go with them, that no harm may befall them from anyone; that they may complete their journey and voyage in perfect security.

We pray thee for the afflicted, in prison and in poverty; sustain them all, free them from their bonds and from their poverty, comfort them all, thou who art the Comfort and the Consolation.

We pray thee for the sick; grant them health and the cure of their sickness; give them perfect health of body and soul, for thou art the Saviour and the Benefactor, thou art the Lord and King of all.

We have prayed to thee for all, through thy only-begotten Jesus Christ, through whom is given to thee the glory and the power, in holy Spirit, now and for ever. Amen.

Blessing of the Layfolk

May the living and the pure hand, the hand of the Only-begotten, the hand which removes all our evils and brings us holiness and protection, be stretched over the bowed heads of this people.

May there descend upon them the blessing of the Spirit, the blessing of heaven, the blessing of the prophets and apostles, that it may guard their bodies for purity and chastity, their souls for learning and knowledge and the mysteries.

May all together be blessed by thy only-begotten Jesus Christ, through whom is given to thee the glory and the power, in holy Spirit, now and for ever. Amen.

Prayer for the sick

We beseech thee, Overseer, Lord and Fashioner of the body and Creator of the soul, who hast formed man, who dost administer, govern and save the whole human race, who in thy goodness dost reconcile and appease; be merciful, O Lord, help and heal all the sick, rebuke the sicknesses, raise up those who are prostrate, glorify thy holy name, through thine only-begotten Jesus Christ: through whom is given to thee the glory and the power in holy Spirit, now and for ever. Amen.

Blessing of the sick

Lord, God of mercies, stretch out thy hand to heal all the sick; make them worthy to be healed; deliver them from their present sickness. Let them be healed in the name of thy Only-begotten; may his holy name be to them a remedy to make them healthy and sound, for through him is given to thee the glory and the power, now and for ever. Amen.

Prayer for the fruits of the earth

Creator of heaven and earth, thou hast adorned the sky with a crown of stars and illuminated it with the sun and the moon, thou hast adorned the earth with its fruits for the service of men; thou hast willed that mankind, created by thee, should rejoice in the bright shining of the sun and moon and be nourished by the fruits of the soil; we beseech thee to send us rains in great abundance and grant to the earth rich harvests and great fertility, because of thy goodness and lovingkindness.

Remember those who have recourse to thee; may thy holy and only Catholic Church be honoured; hear our prayers and supplications and bless the whole earth, through thy only-begotten Jesus Christ, through whom is given to thee the glory and the power, in holy Spirit, for ever and ever. Amen.

Prayer for the Church

O Lord, God of the ages, God of rational spirits, God of pure souls and of all who invoke thee in sincerity and purity, in heaven thou art made known and manifested to pure spirits, on earth thou art hymned and dwellest in the Catholic Church; holy angels and pure souls praise thee, and thou hast made of the very heavens a living choir to the glory and praise of the truth; grant to thy Church to be living and pure, to have heavenly powers and pure angels to serve it, that it may be able to hymn thee in purity.

We pray thee for all the members of this Church; grant to all reconciliation, pardon and the forgiveness of all their sins. Help them not to sin again, be a wall to them and remove every temptation.

Have mercy on men, women and children; reveal thyself to all; may the knowledge of thee be written in their hearts: we ask it through thy only-begotten Jesus Christ, through whom is given to thee the glory and the power, in holy Spirit, for ever and ever. Amen.

BLESSINGS

(The various offerings are distinct from the Eucharist, and there are special blessings for each. Besides oil, cheese and olives, the following are offered and blessed: "grapes, figs, pomegranates, pears, apples, mulberries, peaches, cherries and almonds," besides roses and lilies among the flowers.

Blessing of oil

O God, who sanctifies oil and givest it for the health of those who use and receive it; who hast thereby given anointing to kings, priests and prophets, grant that it may likewise bestow strength on those who receive it and health on those who use it.

Blessing of cheese and olives

Sanctify this solidified milk and solidify us also in charity. Grant that this fruit of the olive may never lose its sweetness, for it is the symbol of the abundance thou hast made to flow from the tree (*sc.* the cross), for all who put their trust in thee.

Blessing of new fruits

We thank thee, O God, and we offer thee the firstfruits which thou hast given us to enjoy and hast produced by thy word, bidding the earth bring forth all kinds of fruits, to refresh and feed mankind and all the beasts.

We praise thee, O God, for all these gifts and for all

the benefits thou hast bestowed on us, adorning all creation with divers fruits, through thy Son Jesus Christ our Lord, through whom thou art glorified for ever and ever. Amen.

The prayer of the Lucernarium

The Jews, on Friday and Saturday evenings, performed the blessing of the lamp, to mark the beginning and end of the sabbath. This rite inspired the Christian ceremony of the Lucernarium which, with the blessing of the lamp, constituted a thanksgiving for the day.

In the evening, when the bishop is present, the deacon brings in a lamp. The bishop, standing in the midst of the people, at the time of thanksgiving, first gives the greeting, saying:

The Lord be with you all.
The people answer: And with thy spirit.
Bishop: Let us give thanks to the Lord.
People: It is meet and right. To him are due greatness and majesty and glory.
(*The bishop does not say: "Lift up your hearts," for that will be said at the time of the oblation.*)
He prays: We thank thee, O God, through thy servant Jesus Christ, our Lord, for enlightening us, by showing us the incorruptible light.

The day is over and we have come to the fall of night. We have been gladdened by the light of day which thou hast created for our joy.

And now that we lack not light for the evening, we hymn thy holiness and glory, through thy only Son, Jesus Christ, our Lord, through whom is given to thee, with him and the Holy Spirit, glory, power and honour, now and for ever and ever.
And all say: Amen.

THE PRAYER OF ST GENESIUS OF ROME[1]

Racked on the wooden horse, long torn with iron spikes, burned with torches, he persevered in confessing his faith, saying:

There is no king save him whom I have seen. Him I adore, to him I do homage. Were I slain a thousand times for giving him worship, I should still be faithful to him as now. Christ's name is on my lips, Christ is in my heart, no tortures can tear it from him. I repent of my past errors; I repent that I once reviled that name, held holy by all holy men. I repent that I have come so late, as a presumptuous soldier, to adore the true King.

CHRISTIAN DEATH

Maximilian (near Carthage, A.D. 295)

In the consulship of Tuscus and Anulinus, on the 12th of March, at Thoveske, Fabius Victor was brought before the court, with Maximilian. Pomeianus, attorney for the treasury, spoke first: "Fabius Victor, tax-collector, is before the court with Valerian Quintian, imperial commissioner, along with the conscript Maximilian, Victor's son. As Maximilian is probably liable for military service, I request that his height be measured."

Dion the proconsul said to the conscript: "What is your name?"

Maximilian: Why do you want to know my name? I am not allowed to serve. I am a Christian.

Proconsul: Put him under the measure.

While they were doing this, Maximilian said: "I cannot serve: I cannot do wrong; I am a Christian."

[1] Genesius had been an actor at Rome, but while acting a parody of baptism he was converted by grace. He is said to have been executed under Diocletian, about 285.

Proconsul: Measure him.

Which done, the assistant announced "Five feet, ten inches."

Proconsul: Mark him.

Maximilian resisted, saying: "I refuse; I cannot serve."

Proconsul: He must either serve or die.

Maximilian: I will not be a soldier. You can cut my head off, but I refuse to serve in the armies of this world. I am a soldier of my God.

Proconsul: Who has put these ideas in your head?

Maximilian: My conscience, and he who has called me.

The proconsul then said to Victor, the young man's father: "Give him some good advice!"

Victor: He is old enough to know his duty.

Proconsul (to Maximilian): Be a soldier and accept the leaden seal, the sign of enlistment.

Maximilian: I have nothing to do with your sign. I already bear the sign of Christ, my God.

Proconsul: I am going to send you to join your Christ, here and now.

Maximilian: That is all I ask. That will be glory for me.

Dion the proconsul said to the assistants; "Mark him!" Maximilian answered as he struggled: "I refuse to accept the sign of the world. If you put it on me by force, I will tear it off, for it is worth nothing. I am a Christian. I can never wear this seal, for I wear the sign of salvation I received from my Lord Jesus Christ, the Son of the living God. You do not know him: he suffered for our salvation and God delivered him for our sins. He is the one we serve, all we Christians. He is the one we follow as the guide of our lives and the author of our salvation."

Proconsul: Become a soldier and take the sign: if not, you will die a shameful death.

Maximilian: I shall not die! My name is already written down with my God. I cannot be a soldier.

Proconsul: Think of your youth and become a soldier. It is a fine life for a young man!

Maximilian: My service is under my God. I have already told you, I cannot serve the world. I am a Christian.

Proconsul: In the bodyguard of our lords Diocletian and Maximilian, Constantius and Maximus, there are Christian soldiers, and they serve.

Maximilian: That is their business. I only know I am a Christian and I cannot do wrong.

Proconsul: But those who serve—what wrong do they do?

Maximilian: You know very well what they do.

Proconsul: Come on, now, be a soldier! If you refuse military service, you will have to die.

Maximilian: I shall not die, not I! If I leave this world, my soul lives on with Christ, my Lord.

Proconsul: Strike his name off.

When his name was struck off the proconsul said: "Since you have insubordinately refused to serve in the army, you shall suffer the penalty of the law. Let this be an example to others!" He read out his sentence on the tablet: "Maximilian, out of insubordination, has refused the military oath and is therefore condemned to die by the sword."

Maximilian: Thanks be to God!

He was twenty-one years old, three months and eighteen days.

On the way to execution Maximilian said: "My dear brothers, make haste with all the strength of your desires to win to the sight of the Lord, that you too may deserve the crown!" Then, with radiant face, he said to his father: "Give the executioner my new suit, the one you had made for my army service. My reward will be increased a hundred-fold when I welcome you in heaven. Then we shall sing the praises of the Lord together."

And speedily he consummated his martyrdom.

A matron called Pomeia obtained leave from the magistrate to take away the martyr's body. She placed it in her litter and brought it to Carthage, where she buried it, near the Palace, not far from the Martyr Cyprian. Twelve days later she too died and was laid to rest in the same place.

As for Victor, Maximilian's father, he went home full of joy, thanking God that he had been able to offer such a gift to the Lord, and very soon he was reunited to him.

Thanks be to God! Amen.

Marcellus (at Tangiers, A.D. 298)

First examination

At Leda, under the government of Fortunatus the prefect, when the emperor's birthday was being celebrated, in the middle of the festivities, Marcellus, one of the centurions, declared that he would have nothing to do with heathen banquets. He threw his sword-belt on the ground in front of the legion's standards which were erected there, and made an open profession of faith: "I am a soldier of Jesus Christ, the eternal King. Henceforth I refuse to serve your emperors. I scorn to worship your gods of wood and stone, which are idols, deaf and dumb."

These words astounded all those present. The soldiers seized him and put him under close arrest. A report was sent to the commander, Fortunatus, who had the centurion put in prison. When the feasting was over, he ordered him to be sent to the consistory.

Marcellus the centurion was brought in and Anastasius Fortunatus said to him: "Why did you throw off your belt, your baldric and your vine-switch, in violation of military discipline?"

Marcellus: On the 21st of July, in presence of the standards of your legion, when you were celebrating your emperor's birthday, I declared publicly and loudly that I was a Christian, that I could not take the oath and serve under any standards but those of Jesus Christ, the Son of God the Father almighty.

Fortunatus: The charge is too serious for me to pass over, I am obliged to refer it to the emperors and to Caesar. I shall transfer you to my superior, Aurelius Agricolanus, Deputy for the Prefect of the Guard. You will be handed over to the care of Caecilius.

Second interrogation

On the 30th of October, Marcellus appeared at Tangiers.

The clerk of the court began: "The centurion Marcellus is transferred to our court by the prefect Fortunatus. Here is his report. Is it to be read?"

Agricolanus agreed and the clerk proceeded to read: "From Fortunatus, to you, my lord, etc. . . ."

When it was read, Agricolanus asked: "Did you say the words alleged in the prefect's report?"

Marcellus: I did.

Agricolanus: Were you a centurion, on regular service?

Marcellus: I was.

Agricolanus: What madness possessed you to throw off your military badges and say such words?

Marcellus: There is no madness in those who fear God.

Agricolanus: Did you say all the words alleged in the report?

Marcellus: I did.

Agricolanus: Did you throw off your badges?

Marcellus: I did, for it is not right for a Christian who is a soldier of Christ to serve in the armies of the world.

Agricolanus: The actions of Marcellus are subject to military discipline. "Inasmuch as Marcellus, being on regular service, was guilty in public of renouncing his military allegiance and moreover, in the course of his trial, spoke seditious words, we order him to be put to death by the sword."

While he was being led to execution Marcellus said: "May God bless you. Agricolanus!"

Thus he departed this world, a glorious martyr.

Euplus (*at Catania in Sicily,* A.D. *304*)

In the ninth consulate of Diocletian and the eighth of Maximian, on the 12th of August, at Catania:

Euplus the deacon, standing before the curtain which shuts off the secretariat of the court, shouted: "I am a Christian: I wish to die for the name of Christ."

Hearing this the governor said: "Bring in the man who said that." So Euplus was brought into the audience-chamber, carrying the book of the Gospels in his hands.

Maximus, a friend of Calvinian the governor, said: "This man ought not to keep such writings: it is forbidden by the imperial decree." Calvinian said to Euplus: "Where do you get these books? From your home?"

Euplus: I have no home. My Lord Jesus Christ knows that well.

The governor: Was it you who brought these books here?

Euplus: Surely you saw me carrying them when I came in.

The governor: Read to us from them.

Euplus: "Blessed are those who suffer justice for justice's sake," he read, and again, "If any man wishes to be my disciple, let him take up his cross and follow me."

When Calvinian had heard these and other passages like them, he asked: "What does that mean?"

Euplus: It is the law of my Lord, as it has been taught to me.

The governor: By whom?

Euplus: By Jesus Christ, the Son of the living God.

The governor interrupted him, saying: "His admission

is explicit. Let him be questioned under torture; hand him over to the torturers."

So Euplus was handed over to the torturers, and the second interrogation began while he was being tortured.

In the ninth consulate of Diocletian and eighth of Maximian, on the 12th of August, Calvinian the governor said to Euplus, who was being tortured, "Do you still stick to the admissions you made just now in your confession?" Euplus signed his forehead with his free hand and answered: "What I confessed, I still confess. I am a Christian, and I read the divine Scriptures."

The governor: Why have you kept these books in your possession? The emperors have forbidden them. You ought to have given them up to the authorities.

Euplus: Because I am a Christian: I am not allowed to give them up. Sooner would I die than give them up. They contain eternal life. If a man gives them up, he loses eternal life. So as not to lose that, I lay down my life.

Calvinian interrupted: "Let Euplus be tortured, then. He has not given up the Scriptures as our rulers ordered, but has read them to the people."

In the midst of his torments Euplus repeated: "I thank thee, O Christ; keep me, for I am suffering for thee."

The governor: Euplus, give up this madness! Worship the gods, and you shall have your freedom!

Euplus: I worship Christ: I detest your demons. Do what you like; I am a Christian. I have long wished for these torments. Do what you will; increase my torments, if you like: I am a Christian.

The governor: Wretched fellow! Worship the gods! Honour Mars, Apollo, Aeculapius!

Euplus: I worship the Father and the Son and the Holy Ghost. I worship the Blessed Trinity; there is no other God. Perish all idols, which have not created heaven or earth, but merely dwell in them! I am a Christian.

The governor: If you would save your life, offer sacrifice!
Euplus: I do; but it is myself I am offering in sacrifice,
to Christ my God. I have nothing more to sacrifice to
him. Your attempts are in vain. I am a Christian.

Calvinian ordered the tortures to be resumed, more
cruelly than before. In the midst of his torments Euplus
repeated: "I thank thee, O Christ; come to my help, O
Christ. It is for thee I am suffering, O Christ." He kept
on repeating these prayers, and when his strength was
exhausted and he had no voice left, his failing lips continued to form these and other such petitions.

Then Calvinian withdrew to dictate the sentence. Soon
he returned with the tablet and read out: "Inasmuch as
Euplus, the Christian, has disobeyed the emperor's edict,
blasphemed the gods and refused to recant, I command
that he be beheaded with the sword. Let him be led out."

Filled with joy, Euplus kept repeating: "Thanks be to
Christ, our God!" He hastened his steps, as if walking to
his crowning. Arrived at the place of execution, he knelt
down and prayed for a long time and again gave thanks
to God. Then he offered his head to the headsman and
was beheaded.

Later on, the Christians came to remove his body, and
after embalming it they buried it.

SELECT BIBLIOGRAPHY

(An asterisk denotes works by non-Catholics)

NOTE ON TRANSLATION OF TEXTS. For all contemporary documents in this book the translator has followed the interpretation of the author, Professor Zeiller, or his collaborators, MM. A. Hamann and F. Amiot. But wherever possible the translator has checked these versions by reference to standard English translations taken from the following collections:

QUASTEN, J. and PLUMPE, J. C., Editors: *Ancient Christian Writers* series, volumes 1 and 6. London, Longmans and Westminster, Md, Newman Press, 1946 and 1948.

*BETTENSON, H.: *The Early Christian Fathers,* London and New York, Oxford Univ. Press, 1956.

*CRESSWELL, R. H. (Editor): *The Liturgy of the Eighth Book of the Apostolic Constitutions,* London, S.P.C.K., 1924.

*DIX, GREGORY: *The Treatise of the Apostolic Tradition of St Hippolytus of Rome,* London, S.P.C.K. (for Church Historical Society), 1938.

*KIDD, B. J.: *Documents Illustrative of the History of the Church,* London, S.P.C.K., volume I, 1938.

*OWEN, E. C. E.: *Some Authentic Acts of the Early Martyrs,* London, S.P.C.K., 1927.

*STEVENSON, J.: *A New Eusebius* (a revision of Kidd above), London, S.P.C.K. and New York, Macmillan, 1957.

*WORDSWORTH, J.: *Bishop Sarapion's Prayerbook,* London, S.P.C.K., 1923.

In this series:

BRUNOT, Amédée, S.C.J.: *St Paul and His Message.*

CRISTIANI, Léon: *Heresies and Heretics.*

CAYRÉ, F., A.A.: *The First Spiritual Writers.*

ALTANER, B.: *Patrology,* London and New York, Nelson, 1960.

BARDY, G.: *The Church at the End of the First Century*, London, Sands, 1938.

BATIFFOL, P.: *Primitive Catholicism*, London and New York, Longmans, 1931.

*CARRINGTON, P.: *The Early Christian Church*, Cambridge and New York, 1957.

*DAVIES, J. G.: *Daily Life in the Early Church* and *Social Life of the Early Christians*, London, Lutterworth Press, and New York, Allenson, 1952.

DELEHAYE, H., Bollandist: *The Legends of the Saints* (translated from the first French edn. by V. M. Crawford), London and New York, Longmans, 1907.

HERTLING, Ludwig, S.J.: *A History of the Catholic Church*, London, Peter Owen, 1958 and Westminster, Md., Newman Press, 1957.

HUGHES, P.: *A History of the Church*, Volume I, *The Church and the World in Which It Was Founded*, London and New York, Sheed and Ward, 1946; *Popular History of the Catholic Church*, revised edn., London, Burns Oates, 1958.

*JALLAND, T. G.: *The Origin and Evolution of the Christian Church*, London, Hutchinson and New York, Rinehart, 1950.

*KIDD, B. H.: *A History of the Church to A.D. 461*, London and New York, Oxford Univ. Press, 1922.

LEBRETON, J., and ZEILLER, J.: *The History of the Primitive Church*, four volumes, London, Burns Oates and New York, Macmillan, 1942–8.

*OULTON, J. and CHADWICK, H. (editors): *Alexandrian Christianity*, London, S.C.M. and Philadelphia, Westminster Press, 1954.

POURRAT, P.: *Christian Spirituality*, volume I, London, Burns Oates, 1922, and Westminster, Md., Newman Press, 1953.

QUASTEN, J.: *Patrology*, volumes I and II, Westminster, Md., Newman Press, 1950 and 1953.

*SRAWLEY, J. H.: *The Early History of the Liturgy*, Cambridge, Cambridge Univ. Press and New York, Macmillan, 1947.

*WAND, J. W. C.: *A History of the Early Church to A.D. 500*, London, Methuen, and New York, British Book Centre, 1949.

WARD, Maisie: *Early Church Portrait Gallery*, London and New York, Sheed and Ward, 1959.

The Twentieth Century Encyclopedia of Catholicism

The number of each volume indicates its place in the over-all series and not the order of publication.

All titles are subject to change.

Date Due

OCT 1 8 1976		
DEC 1 2 1980		
DE 14 '84		
FE 20 '85		
DE 5 '87		
PRINTED	IN U. S. A.	